PRAISE FOR *WINNING AT LIVING* AND KURT KRUEGER

"The mind distorts our words and our bodies. We can work tirelessly on saying the right things, doing the right things, and refining our words and actions to fit our goals and values. But until we fix our hearts it will make little difference. The interesting thing is, once we fix our hearts, all sorts of words and actions can be effective in the world. The path to what we seek lies first in fixing our hearts and minds, not in arranging our words or actions. This book provides the evidence for this powerful truth, and teaches us a path to get there—it presents that argument and how to do it superbly. Thanks for sharing it."

—AMANDA MCCARTHY

Parent of three children and a wife, teacher of Shakespeare,

Director, mentor to high school students

"You did a wonderful job with Bajaj Electrical's Select Employees and Management Team. You related modern research with ancient wisdom to not only feel better but do better. The results were magical. Thank you."

—RAMAKRISHNA BAJAJ

Chairman, Bajaj Group, India

Graham Moss, coach of the Claremont Professional Football Club of Western Australia said: "One strong reason we took second in the Grand Final (like the Super Bowl for Australian Rules Football) was using the ISP practices."

After just three months, American high school student Greg Denby, a high jumper with a personal best of 6'6", leapt 7'1" (and) wrote: "Mr. Krueger taught me two practices that helped make me jump higher than I had ever thought I could." He received a Division I university scholarship!

Patrick Chappel of South Africa, Cape to Rio racer wrote, "Just briefly, very well done last night! It was super fun, interesting and a thought-provoking presentation. I think everyone benefited enormously including myself. It's not easy—actually very difficult—to change the way one thinks and I think you picked away at a lot of the mental blockades and conventional thought processes many of us have. Well done again!"

Anita Sood of Bombay (Mumbai), India, who set eight national swimming records, said "These practices of the Institute of Sports Psychology made me be so much better and broke down so many barriers that I convinced Mr. Krueger to personally train the Indian Team for the Asian Games in Delhi."

Adrian Carter, Sports Director, Witwatersrand University, Johannesburg, speaking about the public Peak Performance

Practices program: "Personally- I enjoyed it as I realize personally when I was younger as a sportsman how much better I could have been had these skills been imparted on me. From the collective, this country is sorely lacking these skills."

Here's a recent endorsement by Caroline Wolsky, a teacher in Los Angeles Unified School District. She took a professional development class, Peak Performance for the Academics and Sports:

"Just wanted to let you know that I stopped drinking soda the moment you lead me through the Switching® exercise, I think it was four or five weeks ago now. When I got to my car after class that night, I had a soda waiting in my cup holder. I tossed it out and immediately and called my husband to let him know that I no longer drink soda.

"I was drinking a minimum of 12 ounces of diet cola a day and often closer to 32 ounces. I have absolutely no desire to start drinking soda of any kind again. Thank you for the many gifts you bestowed upon all of us!"

WINNING
WAYS *for* LIVING

BOOKS BY KURT KRUEGER

WINNING WAYS for LIVING
Get Smarter ~ Perform Better
THREE BOOKS in ONE
Mind • Body • Spirit

WINNING WAYS for LIVING
Get Smarter ~ Perform Better
BOOK 1 ~ Mind

WINNING WAYS for LIVING
Get Smarter ~ Perform Better
BOOK 2 ~ Body

WINNING WAYS for LIVING
Get Smarter ~ Perform Better
BOOK 3 ~ Spirit

WINNING
WAYS *for* LIVING

GET SMARTER ~ PERFORM BETTER

THREE BOOKS IN ONE

MIND • BODY • SPIRIT

KURT KRUEGER

Founder of Success Systems International

and the Institute of Sports Psychology

SUCCESS SYSTEMS INTERNATIONAL

For information about special discounts for bulk purchases
or author interviews, appearances, and speaking engagements
please contact Kurt Krueger through the website below::

www.SuccessSystemsInternational.net

First Edition

Manuscript development, editing, cover and book design by
Rodney Miles: www.RodneyMiles.com

Cover image, *The Matterhorn seen from the Domhütte (Valais):*
https://en.wikipedia.org/wiki/Matterhorn#/media/File:Matt
erhorn_from_Domh%C3%BCtte_-_2.jpg, and
sunset_over_mountains_near_sea_by_macinivnw-d68mz45

Dedicated to God first,

then to family,

and to the community of seekers of truth—

that's *you*!

How are You the Hope of Humanity?

I HAVE A QUEST

Do you?

There's plenty of *fear* and *hate* in the world—too much.

Let's release people from suffering the poverty of the soul and pocketbook. This quest has led me over the past 45 years to seek the answers. I got to serve the poor. I got to share the joys of the heart. I got to laugh. Most importantly, I got to let go and let God.

My prayer for you today is:

That you receive all that you heartily desire. Let this book and life give you MORE!

Learn the bliss of Self-help. You may *then* more easily help others.

You are the Hope of Humanity. You are unique! Thank you for your loving energy.

Always be happy. Enjoy the Bliss of Freedom in this incredible Play of Consciousness.

Love,

—KURT, PHD = "PLAY HAPPILY DAILY"

CONTENTS

A NOTE TO READERS

IN MY YEARS OF RESEARCH AND TEACHING, the methods you are about to be exposed to have been used most visibly by athletes and business people who have results that are both demonstrable and dramatic. However, I do not take for granted those results that occur perhaps a little more quietly, yet nonetheless just as significantly and importantly, within the hearts and minds of students, and those that become the happy tools of teachers. After a fulfilling and rewarding teaching career of my own, it may be the student who finds these tools and techniques to be of great help to him or her in *learning* that I cherish most of all. So as you read the pages that follow and as you learn and apply the methods you discover herein, my wish for you is an easier, happier, and more wonderful experience in your own lifelong love of learning. A tremendous amount of *fear* and *anger* experienced today may be relieved a good deal when one practices the techniques of *Winning Ways for Living*. At some point, I hope you will reach me, and tell me all about it.

—Kurt Krueger

November 8, 2016

Kagel Canyon, California

BOOK ONE ~ MIND

"Life is either a daring adventure, or nothing."

—HELEN KELLER

Introduction: Discovering Winning Ways

> "Stop wasting time playing a role or concept. Instead, learn to actualize yourself— your potential."
>
> —Bruce Lee

MY LIFE CHANGED on a sunny California day. It was the spring of 1966 and I was competing in the state community college swim championships. Up to that day my best time was a 1:08 (one minute eight seconds) for the 100-yard breaststroke, as an average swimmer at Los Angeles Valley College. We were competing against our arch-rival from Northern California, Foothill College, and I swam a 1:05.2 (one-minute, five and two tenths seconds) in the prelim's. This resulted in a swim-off against a fast 1:04 Foothill swimmer.. I blew the guy out of the water, swimming a 1:03.7 race, and became an All-American swimmer.

This earned me a scholarship to the University of Colorado, where I went on to set three school records. For years I tried to discover how I was able to drop to a 1:03.7 from a 1:08 in such a short time. I searched the literature on peak performance. I looked in both Eastern and Western psychology. I investigated all the leads I could find for achieving a peak experience, finally coming up with a synthesis and a system. It took nearly 30 years of experimenting with myself. During these 30-plus years, I also taught teachers, students, corporate executives, and others what was working, with great results. This all helped to produce *Winning Ways for Living*. There are ancient secrets as well as modern methodologies included. You may have already tried some. You may be new to others. You will find many to be simple, and they are—simple and effective.

Since that day as a young man, I have learned many secrets. Swami Muktananda of Ganeshpuri, India was the primary source. I took a one-year sabbatical from teaching in 1974 and lived and studied in India. I practiced daily meditation and concentration techniques, attended classes, and studied. I worked to support the ashram. I ate well, and did yogic exercises. I investigated and lived according to the Indian philosophy, psychology, and culture. I wanted to incorporate these into my teaching of high school world history when I got home.

Swami Muktananda was a short elderly man, and he normally dressed in bright clothes. He used to say, "The kingdom of heaven dwells within." He also offered the discovery of abilities, knowledge, and practices to fully experience that kingdom. He taught us to eat and exercise properly so the Temple of the Soul, as Plato said, was fit for the spirit. He taught us to pray so we could talk to God. He had us meditate so we could listen to God. He taught us to think good thoughts so we would be positive channels for grace to flow into our every action. Along with these teachings he constantly instructed us to:

- Apply this knowledge to our everyday life,

- Begin seeing God in each other more and more,

- Understand that total power and knowledge is latent within us, and

- Seek the ultimate first, and that all will then follow.

The techniques he taught are very powerful and effective. They need discrimination for dissemination. Muktananda said it was time everyone knew their own true nature. It needed to be applied for daily living. I first began applying Muktananda's techniques myself during my time as a junior high school teacher. I was teaching in the inner city of Los Angeles and the school was one of the worst in America at the time. It had the two biggest black and Latino gangs in the country! I taught social studies, history, and geography in a bungalow separated from the main campus by the physical education and shop buildings. It was surrounded by the basketball courts and football and baseball areas. Students came to class through what was called "the canyon." It was where some dramatic things used to happen—drugs could be acquired, and fights often broke out. Students often did not come into the class in a frame of mind conducive for learning.

I asked my students to quietly come into the class while they got their materials out for the day. They would then sit quietly with their eyes and mouths closed. During those two-to-five minutes each day, they focused on the sound of their breath. They were told that this would bring the power of concentration to their mind. This could thereby positively affect their abilities in school. It also had a calming effect for their stimulated glands. This application worked so well that they improved their grades in social studies and other subjects, too. And it was easy to have these active "crazy kids" do this—I simply demanded it as any good teacher would.

A couple of weeks later, I asked them to use a mantra. I explained, 'The mantra focuses the mind even faster as you repeat a chosen set of words along with the breath. When your brain calms down, your heart rate calms down as well, and concentration happens the quickest as you calm the breath with the mantra. I told them, "Please repeat OM NA-MAH SHI-VA-YA, as you breathe in and out. It means 'I honor my inner Self,' or 'I bow to Shiva.' It is a phrase that has been used for thousands of years by millions of people each year."

One student we called Big John, a 6'4," 240-pound 8th grade student, challenged me on this one day, shouting, "What do you mean, say OM NAMA who? I ain't gonna do that."

"John," I said, "I don't know if you're repeating OM NA-MAH SHI-VA-YA, I do know that your eyes and mouth are closed. You now know why it is better to use OM NA-MAH

SHI-VA-YA, so it's your choice. Try and give your mind a rest. Let your body relax. Give yourself a nice restful break. It will help improve your grades." I continued to require it of the whole class, and if students began to lose focus during a class, I would call out, "Number one!" (I now suggest saying the word 'Shakti,' as it means energy) and they would immediately sit up straight and close their mouths and eyes while focusing on the breath, until instructed to begin work again. This is better than some other commands teachers may frequently use, as it has the ability to calm them and it focused the class while energizing them for learning. Only when calm permeated the room would we continue with the lesson.

And I would soon need what I was teaching in a situation of my own, a situation of life and death. Thank God it followed that year long trip to India.

ON A FATEFUL TUESDAY MORNING in Bombay, India, on September 27, 1977, I walked onto the Japan Airlines flight bound for Los Angeles via Tokyo. I was tired from the two-hour early morning delay. I sat reflectively in my economy seat. It had been a wonderful year studying the intricate psychology, culture, and philosophy of India. I had lived in a tiny village Ashram[1] in Ganeshpuri, some 65 miles northeast of Bombay. It seemed like I could still smell the mellowing fragrance of the tropical flowers. The year had been transformative. I'd had time for myself, time to reflect on my understanding of life, to reflect about my love of teaching, and about new ways for reaching my students and

---

[1] "a spiritual hermitage or a monastery in Indian religions" — https://en.wikipedia.org/wiki/Ashram

tapping into human potential in general. I knew this year was special—I didn't know there were more intense moments in store for me throughout that day. For some 30 to 45 minutes after takeoff, I pondered my daily walks through the gardens of Gurudev Siddha Peeth and the peaceful, early morning meditations punctuated by the shrieking of peacocks. I reflected upon learning from a real master of life and education as I had.

Suddenly, I was shocked back into the reality of the present by shouting on the plane. Five men dressed in pinstripe suits ran down the aisle shouting in some unrecognizable language—*we were being hijacked.* For five minutes we waited, our imaginations running wild, hoping maybe to find Rambo on board to save us or planning to escape alive by leaping from the plane upon landing. Many feared another disaster like when the Japanese Red Army shot up the Tel Aviv airport just a year or so earlier. I knew this was the time to apply the mind control techniques I had learned that year from a master of meditation and yoga, Swami Muktananda. I needed to put it to use in this intense situation. We had five crazed men with automatic weapons, hand grenades, and plastic explosives. We had to hold our hands behind our heads for 45 minutes. This became extremely uncomfortable. I asked politely that we be allowed to put our hands down. The hijacker in charge of our section shakily replied, "No!" as he brandished his automatic handgun in my direction. But soon the chief hijacker allowed us to rest our arms. We were instructed to give them our weapons and other select items. We were allowed to keep our medicine, valuables, and money.

I began to practice a special concentration technique. It was practiced daily in Muktananda's ashram. My state of mind became calm and peacefully meditative. Four hours elapsed before we started our descent. Passengers and hijackers alike were greatly stressed at this dangerous time, yet I had a calm mind. I observed near panic on both sides of the weapons. They had put an older lady in the wing door seat next to me. She began to shake and have irregular breathing. I reached over, gently grabbing her hand. I said, "Calm down, everything will be okay, the Lord is taking care of us!" And she did! My own body then began moving with her symptoms. The hijackers removed me from the seat. They placed me on the floor in the first class section. My breathing stopped at this point. The lady above me shouted, "Help him, he's having a heart attack!" I received closed-heart massage, nitroglycerin, a shot for heart attack, and oxygen. My mind had been calm up to this point. Now it began thinking, "Will this hurt me?"

I had seen people moved like this in meditation intensives. It was caused by the powerful inherent spirit. Inwardly, I queried, "If nothing is wrong with my body, will this hurt me?" A few minutes of these mental gymnastics passed. I was then able to relax again into a calm frame of mind. I remembered what I'd said to the lady: "Calm down, everything will be okay. The Lord is taking care of us." Twenty-six hours after the hijacking started, it ended for me. Some of us were released in Dacca, Bangladesh, and all the rest were released safely over the next five days. It took three days before I was back home in Los Angeles. I found out that I had no damage to my heart, and I began teaching social studies at an inner-city high school.

THREE DAYS LATER another stressful situation arose when I noticed two students fighting in the hall. One was swinging steel pipes in his fists at his opponent. I quickly jumped onto the aggressor, grabbing his arms. Making one pipe drop, I told him to stop. He continued to struggle, so I threw him to the floor and relieved him of his other weapon. The security guard soon took them away. A group had gathered to view the ruckus, including teachers. A couple of teachers went into the faculty lounge to calm down after the incident because they were so affected they could not teach that period. I went back into the classroom and began a government lesson, using the fight as an introduction to a conflict resolution section. I did not feel the rigors and tensions of teaching in a so-called ghetto to be a burden on my psyche or body because of practicing what is contained here, in *Winning Ways.*

Faculty members noticed my calm demeanor which was exhibited in handling such an adverse situation and they asked me to advise them on how to better deal with teaching there. I pondered the variety of techniques for mind control and expansion I'd learned from Muktananda. I found that the newest scientific investigations into these age-old practices had proven their validity for stress management and even more. In fact, since 1974, I have practiced a concentration technique throughout my day which helps in competitions, teaching, learning, and in everyday life. I designed a workshop to bring the practices of the East, with the modern scientific support of research, to the teachers of Los Angeles. The holistic techniques for fully living were then applied successfully for personal stress management, for better education, and even developed to assist businesses as well. I then combined it with nutrition, visualization, Hatha Yoga, and meditation to form a workshop program on peak performance practices. *Winning Ways* was offered so successfully around Southern California that word spread. I was asked to give a program in 1980 at Oxford Medical School (UK) and subsequently in1981 at the United Nations in New York City, and I was invited that same year to give a series of workshops for the British Association of National Coaches in England.

During this same period of teaching, I was talked into entering the International Senior Olympics swim competition by my identical twin brother, Ken. The Senior Olympics was an age-group competition for those above the age of 25, and I entered the 200-meter breaststroke. At the championships, I found that one of my competitors had been a regular American Olympian, had been training intensely, and was peaked for the meet. I had not trained for at least 11 years and had only been a community college-level all-American, and my main practices since 1974 had in fact been mostly psychological rather than physical. So I went to a quiet place before the race, sat for meditation, and did a special breathing practice.

At race time I fired off the blocks, swimming intently. At the 100-meter turn, I noticed we were neck-and-neck in the lead, and this is when it happened. I started thinking, "Oh! I went out too fast, I'll die. He's in shape, he will kill me," and so on. Then for the next 50 meters the whole field pulled near or passed me. Then, at the last turn, I remembered the concentration technique and quickly applied it. I began pulling up beyond those who had passed me. In the end, I was beaten by half a body length—the silver medal was mine! In all, during four different competitions, I won eleven gold and five silver medals, all without swim training.

Some track athletes at the high school heard of my success. They asked for my assistance in their sport, so I taught them a meditation and a visualization technique. After three months, a regular 6'6" high jumper went 7'1." Another had been the sixth fastest sprinter with a slow start. He became so much faster that he led off the second fastest sprint relay team in the state of California. Still another student had been a 2:01 (two-minute one second) 880-yard runner who improved to 1:54.

I presented my second international lecture and paper, *Meditation and the Ultimate Performance in Sports* at the 1984 Olympic Scientific Congress. Bob Beamon presented the keynote speech in sport psychology there. He had long-jumped nearly two feet farther than anyone in history during the 1968 Mexico City Olympics, and this had lead the media to create a new term—"Beamonesque," which meant an athletic performance "beyond the beyond," or breaking a world record by a vast margin. **Bob then became a sports psychologist to find out how to repeat the *inner* experience, and he told me that meditation was the state of mind that he was in when he did his jump, and that he only wished he knew how to meditate much earlier in his life.**

THE FIRST PART of the twentieth century saw tremendous advances in physical abilities, triggered by advances in equipment, physiology, training regimens, nutrition, and the beginnings of mental training. The last quarter of the 20th century saw advances in high technology and spiritual trainings being used for enabling people to be all they can be.

We can apply each of these techniques in our own lives. We can then arrange them into a system, which will have a great synergistic effect. This is how the *Winning Ways* system began, after 10 years of development, and what I began to teach in its entirety during 1987. When it has been applied by athletes, they have taken quantum leaps in performance and they have improved themselves mentally, socially, and morally. *Winning Ways* offers methods for using your full body, mind, and spirit so that you will be able to reach your God-given potential. When you follow the techniques you will be able to ascend to new levels of performance in life. Your body will be pure and toned for any performance. Your mind will be clear to function adroitly. You will be in tune with the inner spirit for full energy and knowledge. This is not easy to accomplish—you have to practice and modify your life in thought, word, and deed, but the fruits of your dedicated efforts will be literally unbelievable.

Bejoy Jain, for example, a youthful Indian boy, took a workshop in *Winning Ways* in 1982. The program was six hours in duration, held in Shree Gurudev Ashram. Bejoy took the practices to heart and dedicated himself to self-improvement. He had been a "normal" swimmer in his home town near Bombay. Two weeks later, he set a national junior record in the 100-meter breaststroke. He didn't stop at that, either. Two months later Bejoy swam the English Channel faster than any Asian had. His youthful enthusiasm and dedicated practices were primary contributors to his great success. He's now a famous architect in India.

The intent of this book is to open you to your "Self," to your full capabilities. For example, when the body is properly trained with warm-ups and cool-downs, health and performance are dramatically enhanced. With a practice of *Winning Ways,* a high school football team in Novato, California, went seven years without a person missing a game because of a muscle injury, and six of those years were winning years.

Einstein is said to have used only 10 percent of his brain, which makes me wonder how much I am accessing, as biologists say that at least 90 percent of our brain's capacity goes unused. So what can we do to begin using more brainpower? In *Winning Ways* we learn several methods for physical and mental training, some of which have enabled people to learn languages in just six weeks. Others improve I.Q. levels by 20 points, and competitive performance by 50 percent.

Olympic decathlon gold medalist Bruce Jenner has said, "I always felt that my greatest asset was not my physical ability, it was my mental ability." Elite athletes around the globe have echoed this same idea, from Pele to Tiger Woods, to Serena Williams and Bruce Lee. Like these greats, when you train your body and your mind, you will reach more of your potential. For those involved in working for a living, the benefits include less stress, improved health, creative inspiration, and more. When the spirit is tapped, amazing abilities present themselves. You may have heard of:

- women picking up cars when their child is pinned beneath;

- Philippides running more than 26 miles as fast as possible to Athens to report victory over the Persians;

- mountains being moved by Mohammed, Lao Tzu, and others;

- running for long periods of time, up and down the mountains of Tibet, day or night, by the Lompong runners;

- people not being able to be picked up by the strongest of men;

- and even more "impossible" feats.

The uniqueness of *Winning Ways* is that we open ourselves up to the inherent spirit. It's the source of our energy, enthusiasm, inspiration, intelligence, enjoyment, and so much more. *Winning Ways* is a practical conduit of ancient wisdom for the modern person, and these practices are totally supported by scientific research. Practicing the techniques of *Winning Ways* will strengthen our bodies, expand our minds, harmonize our emotions, and elevate our spirits to new heights, all which enables us, with the grace of dedicated effort, to reach our full potentials.

Some people have taken only a day to reap the benefits. One young college student used a stress management technique learned in a two-weekend course and sailed through a speech in a communications course. One boy took just two weeks before he improved from a good local swimmer to a national junior record holder. The moral here can be illustrated by the story of the Sufi[2], Mulla Nassurdin: Nassurdin: He was walking from Baghdad to Mecca. A pilgrim came alongside him in the hot desert and asked, "Have you traveled to Mecca before?"

"Many times," Nassurdin answered.

The pilgrim responded, "How long will it take me to get to Mecca?"

The wise and venerable Nassurdin answered, "I don't know."

The seeker of Mecca became angry and shouted, "If you have been to the Holy City why don't you tell me how long it will take to get there, or are you just a fakir[3]?"

Nassurdin calmly replied, "I know how long it takes *me* to travel, I don't know your pace." Thus, go at *your* pace in using these practices that will get to your goals.

Executives and leaders in the world all know that a mentally strong individual with a strong body will out-produce another. Consequently, many corporate facilities now contain visual arts, jogging tracks, fitness centers, swimming pools, and organic cafeterias. This brings up a question. If I am doing just physical exercise training, what can I do to train and strengthen my mind? And can these be done simultaneously?

---

[2] "Muslims and mainstream scholars of Islam define Sufism as simply the name for the inner or esoteric dimension of Islam which is supported and complemented by outward or exoteric practices of Islam, such as Islamic law." —Wikipedia

[3] a Muslim (or, loosely, a Hindu) religious ascetic who lives solely on alms. —Google definition. The word Faker is derived from this.

After studying mental training around the world with some of the most eminent teachers, I finally saw how I developed into a national athlete. I remembered back to those days and saw the ways that the coaches and compatriots affected me, both physically and mentally. All too often the mental aspects were subconsciously affected. Neither the coaches nor I knew nor realized that the mind had also been trained. We didn't know there were conscious ways to train the mind to enhance and perfect performance.

You will enjoy the practices and results which will come from applying the knowledge in our book (and this is *our* book, as it can become a part of you in creating your life). Your daily life, vocation, and/or sport will be dramatically improved through regularly practicing *Winning Ways*. Some of us who have gained a certain level of expertise in our fields will find that we have either consciously or unconsciously practiced some of these techniques already. And a synergistic effect takes place when all the *Winning Ways* practices are applied—we gain more energy and abilities than the effort we put into it.

When we approach life in a conscious manner, we will most expeditiously reach our potential. This is the purpose of our book. We will learn about training and opening our body, mind, and spirit for peak performance in our field of endeavor. This exciting new paradigm for fitness and peak performance allows the body, mind, and spirit to be trained for ultimate results:

- Concentration practices bring the mind into focus at will;

- Energy stimulating exercises lead to physical fitness while flexing, toning, and strengthening all bodily systems—exercises that reduce the effects of stress on the body and prevent injury and improve health;

- Stress management prevents the adverse effects stress may have on physical, emotional, and mental performance and health;

- High technology uses innovations for recuperating from health issues and/or injuries, mental fitness and spiritual centering;

- Optimum nutrition leads to physical and mental health, and is shown to improve I.Q. by up to 20 points and endurance and strength by up to 50 percent;

- Visualization, enables one to practice without facilities or equipment, and to implant a blueprint into the mind for perfect movement and performance;

- Affirmations and *afformations* lead to a positive attitude for achieving what we conceive, and reduce fears and anger;

- Meditation accesses the intrinsic spirit and the energy of creativity, enthusiasm, and clarity of thought. It simultaneously overcomes psychological barriers to peak performance.

Let's get started, then—let's be all we can be!

[1] Manage Stress

"If we are peaceful, if we are happy, we can blossom like a flower, and everyone in our family—our entire society will benefit from our peace."

—Thich Nhat Hanh, *Being Peace*

STRESS MANAGEMENT IS NECESSARY in modern life. Some people do great things when there is no pressure, but do not perform well in more stressful situations. Stress may cause them consciously or unconsciously to psych out. The anxiety and tension overpowers them. Stress is defined as a factor that induces bodily or mental tensions (Merriam, 1974). Stress can enter our lives at work, within the family, or while participating in sports—in fact all sports have an element of stress. While there is good stress and bad, stress is normally considered a disagreeable side effect of an active life. The stress of one situation sends you tense into the next, so our lives can be more enjoyable and efficient, and we can have greater energy when we eliminate unnecessary stress.

For example, most people in the world have a fear of speaking in front of groups. This translates into stress-related tensions, such as headaches, nausea, dry mouth, sweaty palms, and so on. It may also cause abnormal communication as compared to a simple dialogue. In sports, as mentioned, you have seen or heard of people who do great things in local or national competitions, yet don't perform as well in bigger events. Divers and gymnasts often successfully perform difficult dives or routines in practice quite regularly, yet during big meets they may just as regularly falter. This is because of the effect stress has on the body and the mind.

But when stress is mitigated or removed, you can more easily soar to greater heights during any situation or competition. Desirable stress management, then, is most effective when we address both body and mind. There are several practices for improvement in these areas, including: meditation, massage, visualization, warm-ups and cool-downs, "Switching®," and others. Learn to channel or overcome stress, and you will have one less obstacle to your full potential.

TYPES OF STRESS

Stress is known to be a major contributor, either directly or indirectly, to accidental injuries, coronary heart disease, cancer, lung ailments, cirrhosis of the liver, and suicide—six of the leading causes of death. The cost to business and industry of stress-related illness, disabilities, accidents and impairments exceeds 150 billion dollars in the United States alone. Stress can cause a missed turn or dive, clear communication in an important meeting, and so much more. The symptoms of (negative) stress in a person take two forms, according to psychologist David Kaus PhD:

- Somatic anxiety is experienced in the body. Examples are muscle spasms, cold or hot hands, butterflies, or nausea. This is caused, whether consciously or unconsciously, by the mind.

- Cognitive anxiety is the worry inside a person's head, resulting in unwanted negative thoughts, fears, worries, inability to concentrate, and other deterrents to performance.

SOMATIC STRESS

Bodily stress also affects the digestive, respiratory, and cardiovascular systems. This stress may manifest itself in nausea, shortness of breath, and rapid heartbeat prior to competition or important meeting. The tension of the muscles may be released by five methods:

(1) Stretching,

(2) The Watusi Jump,

(3) Laughing,

(4) Yawning,

(5) Relaxation or meditation practices.

In essence, stress is brought on by our mental *perception* of a situation. So without the *mental* release of stress, the physical stretching/release will have only partial effect. A highly beneficial practice for stretching and toning the internal and external muscles and the releasing stress is Hatha Yoga. It can be practiced within an individual's capacity. It can be used as a warm-up and a cool-down. Pellitier (1979) found that Hatha Yoga both strengthens and lengthens the muscles. These practices also assist in keeping the mind calm and focused before a performance, thus releasing stress while conserving energy. Hatha Yoga is our preferred method for releasing somatic stress because it is self-inflicted and may be done just about anywhere. With Hatha Yoga we may also choose the areas of the body to be released, including the internal organs. The physiological release of tensions has a corresponding psychological release. Circulation is enhanced thus feeding the brain much needed nutrients. The stretching in Hatha Yoga helps prevent injuries as well.

COGNITIVE STRESS

Mental anxiety and stress is caused by our perception of the world (Pellitier, 1980). The negative thinking process is a culprit in this concern. Overcome cognitive stress by putting the mind—your thoughts—on something other than worries and fears. When one, or preferably each, of these techniques are practiced regularly, psychological stress becomes like a soft breeze, rather than a gale force wind, nicely stimulating our senses for improved performance.

EUSTRESS

And as mentioned, not all stress is bad. Many researchers, including Hans Selye, have described a pleasant form of stress that seems to be invigorating. This pleasant and positively stimulating stress is called "eustress." It is associated with excitement, adventure, and thrilling experiences. This stress is fun, it enhances vital sensations, it "turns on" individuals, and in the process it releases energy. So we don't want to eliminate all stress, we simply want to bring it into its optimum level.

PREVENTING STRESS

We either eliminate, use, or fall victim to stress. Therefore, learn the various symptoms of stress, and learn prevention practices, how to rapidly reduce stress, how to eliminate or mitigate stressors, and learn the means to transform it into a productive advantage. *Winning Ways* employs many methods for all of this:

- Concentration Practices
- "Switching®" (explained in this series)
- Positive Attitude Awareness
- Visualization

- Yoga

- Meditation

- Affirmations

- Afformation

- Visualization

- Routines

- Gratitude

- Blessings

- Forgiveness

- Mindfulness

- Goal/outcome setting

- Various physical activities/fitness practices

- Buddy system—asking for help

- Happiness practices

- Presence in nature—walking, sitting, so on

- And more.

There are various methods for rapid reduction of stress, and we touch on many of these in this series on *Winning Ways:*

- Watusi Jump

- Thymus thumping

- Blessing/Gratefulness

- Calming Breathing

- Removing self/involvement momentarily

- Empathy for perpetrators

- And more.

Dr. Kenneth Pelletier, the prominent stress researcher, notes that of the people he tested, the yogis and experienced meditators had a unique control over their minds and bodies. "They could control their brain waves, their heart rate, blood pressure, skin conductance, muscle tension, peripheral circulation, and respiration pattern and rate. They were all very coherent or balanced, when one went up they all went up . . . the systems that controlled all these very different functions were all very highly integrated." When the yogis and experienced meditators were asked how they learn to control their pulse, for example, they said it was just a matter of practice, like learning a new dive, skill, or musical instrument.

DAILY PRACTICE

When one is fearful, angry, or stressed out, the adrenal glands start producing adrenaline for the "fight or flight" automatic physical response. If we cannot *use* the adrenaline, as while in a car when cut off by another, we need to stop the production of adrenaline because it takes bodily energy to transform it into a "non-toxic" substance, and this prevents you from quickly calming down. Biofeedback and massage are useful tools, to name a few, for reducing somatic stress (Kauss, 1980), but if you are pressed for time, take three complete and deep breaths, or thump the thymus[4] area of the chest a few very firm times. This reduces the overproduction of adrenaline. The "Thymus Thump" quickly helps in a stressful situation, or when in need of an energy boost, or to enhance the immune system. "Thymos" is a Greek word meaning "spiritedness." The Thymus is part of the endocrine system and modulates the production of adrenaline.

After puberty, it begins to slowly atrophy, thus the need to regularly stimulate it each day a few times. The Thymus Thump also stimulates the release of white blood cells (T-lymphocytes) associated with the immune system. The thymus gland is located about two inches beneath the center of your breastbone, at about the third rib, or one hand-width from the base of your throat.

1. With a closed fist, thump the chest (thymus gland) a few firm times while mentally directing the body/mind to relax or to rejuvenate.

2. Take a few deep breaths through your nose (if possible) remembering, "in goes the good air, out goes the bad."

3. Release any tensions in shoulders and abdomen.

---

[4] "The thymus gland, located behind your sternum and between your lungs. —http://www.endocrineweb.com/endocrinology/overview-thymus

4. Refocus on positive thoughts for the next part of your day.

Video: https://www.youtube.com/watch?v=_25L5KKUwC8
See a four-minute video with TWO easy and quick methods to reduce stress in four minutes.

[2] PRIME YOUR MIND

"At the Olympic level the physical capabilities of the competitors are all very close—there are very few physical errors, in fact at that level most are mental errors. Competition at the Olympic level is 80 percent mental challenge and 20 percent physical challenge."

—BRUCE JENNER,

1976 Olympic Decathlon Gold Medal Winner

AFFIRMATIONS

IF YOU DON'T THINK you can, most likely you can't! You can remain a second-class competitor as long as you think you *are* one. But when you start affirming the fact that you *are* great, it can then more readily happen. The winner of eight major PGA championships, Tom Watson said, "Don't hesitate to tell yourself that you are a good putter, even though the evidence suggests otherwise." Think about the baby learning to walk! Building a positive self-image in this matter is vitally important. It keeps you in the proper frame of mind. It allows you to forget your mistakes (or for that matter, shortcomings). You then approach each shot, opportunity, or situation as a fresh challenge. With this attitude, you're bound to be more successful.

Two of the world's great scriptures, the Torah and the Bible offer the same, powerful psychological law for positive thinking in, "As you sow, so shall you reap." The unconscious mind accepts as truth whatever you tell it often enough. When you repeat an idea over and over again, your unconscious mind automatically accepts it as truth. It then sets to work making it a reality in your life. In psychology, this is known as the Law of Predominant Mental Impression. It simply means that you must keep repeating an idea, saying it over so often that it becomes a law for your unconscious mind.

The great African philosopher, Augustine of Hippo wrote, "Faith is to believe what you do not see, and the reward of that faith is to see what you believe." What you conceive, you may achieve. If you really don't believe you can do something, will you even try? So begin using *affirmations*, what we call Positive Attitude Awareness (PAA), to overcome doubt and fear.

Physiologically, remarks that tend to deflate the ego, or discourage a person's efforts, deplete the body's blood-sugar supply and lower a person's vitality and stamina. **Positive Attitude Awareness raises the blood sugar and energy** level *instantly,* **a good reason to start using PAA daily, especially before an important meeting, training, or competition.** Many great sportspeople have applied this awareness to their sport with fantastic results. Mohammad Ali constantly repeated, "I am the greatest!" Pele would think to himself, "Nobody can stop me in futbol (soccer)," and Roger Bannister, the first person to break the four-minute mile repeated, "I will break the four-minute mile." This constant thought forms a habit, the habit forms a character, and the character shapes a destiny. Write down your affirmations. Make each a personal, positive statement in the present tense. It should contain action-emotional words. Write it as though you already have the abilities, like:

"I enjoy feeling healthy."

"I enjoy training intensely."

"Doing a perfect triple somersault feels fantastic."

Practice this technique by saying your affirmation(s) three times in slow motion and from five to 200 times at regular speed or faster. Good times to repeat these affirmations are just before going to bed and upon awakening from sleep—the unconscious mind is most open for consciously programming when you are in a relaxed state of mind. When you repeat the affirmations, imagine yourself experiencing the wonderful feeling of them, and use all your senses for this. Practice them for your personal, sport, school, business, and social life. In just two months of regularly practicing you will have created a wonderful habit and many of the abilities you affirm as well. **The law of cause and effect takes over the**

moment you have a strong idea in mind, and it leads you to take steps that will bring fulfillment.

TRAIN A STRONG MIND

We have all witnessed spontaneous exhibitions of peak performance by "average" people. We have also sadly beheld supremely trained sportspeople dysfunction or psych out. This illustrates the need to approach life and sports from an expanded perspective. No more can we settle for simple physical training alone; the modern efficient person and/or sports person must be satisfactorily trained in:

- Physical functioning—including skills, conditioning, and diet;

- Mental control of anxiety/stress, concentration;

- Inner spirit—the source of inspiration, enthusiasm, energy, and more.

Much like the statement by Bruce Jenner, in Don Shollander's book, *Deep Water* (1971) he observes, "In Olympic competition, a race is won in the mind . . . Winning is 20 percent physical and 80 percent mental." Don was the winner of four gold medals in swimming during the 1964 Tokyo Olympics, and if that was not enough proof, the value of psychological training was evident in a study of four equally matched world-class athletes in the (former) Soviet Union (Garfield, 1984):

- Group I underwent 100% physical training;

- Group II, 75% physical and 25% mental training;

- Group III, 50% physical and 50% mental training; and

- Group IV, 25% physical and 75% mental training.

The significantly greater improvement was exhibited by Group IV, followed by Group III and so on down to the least effectively trained group—Group I. The chief Soviet sports psychologist, V.A. Romanov, summarized their feelings on training thus: "The shaping of psychological readiness is one of the main tasks in preparing athletes for competition." The sage, Swami Muktananda said, "A strong mind is more important than a strong body."

As you know, when you train intensely, yet your mind isn't into competing, you usually don't do so well. Mark E. Schubert, former University of Southern California and American Olympic swim coach, believes in mental training as a key to success. "When the kids get to the national level, they are all just about equal physically." Consequently, much of his focus is on preparing competitors psychologically for upcoming meets, so he uses the services of a sports psychologist.

Indeed, some sports psychologists will give you psychological tests to see where your weaknesses and strengths are, and work from there by counseling you or by giving you a technique or two to practice. Some do research on how you perform according to your psychological profile.

Many sports psychologists will give you two techniques—(1) deep relaxation, which facilitates the next technique, (2) visualization.

[3] VISUALIZE & SET GOALS

"The world is as you see it."

—VASISTHA, from *The Yoga Vasistha*

THE YOGA VASISTHA tells the story of Rama learning how to be King by studying with his Guru, Vasistha, while living in huts in the jungle. Rama, the man/god that Hindus revere as God, was about to return to take over the kingdom from his father. He asked the most important question so far in his studies, "What is your highest teaching?" Vasistha answered, "The world is as you see it!" Psychologists and other scientists are proving this statement so much these days, from quantum scientists to biologists, and more.

Visualization is probably the most used practice in sports psychology. With visualization one can practice a skill perfectly without facilities and/or equipment. It harkens back to our childhood—pretending to be a Knight of the Round Table or queen for a day. Back then we easily imagined that we were animals, off in space, and more. Now is again a good time to "be thee like little children," for peak performance in life, and God willing, beyond! *Winning Vision* (a Way of *Winning Ways*) is seeing with your mind's eye something that will enhance your performance in life. *Winning Vision* techniques enable people in sports, business, education, and the performing arts to:

- Think clearly and rapidly;

- Have directness and sureness of action;

- Create a positive outcome;

- Refine coordination, rhythm, and timing;

- Eliminate physical exertion yet still practice;

- Open energy/nerve channels for precise movements;

- Micro-kinetically actually fire the muscles that are imagined to be moving;

- Release mental constrictions;

- Have the muscles subtly *know* the needful movement;

- Practice a skill perfectly without facilities and/or equipment;

- Relax the mind from fears that could come up beforehand.

TYPES OF VISUALIZATION

There are about 112 methods of *Winning Ways* that deal with visualization that have been developed over the ages, dating back as far as the 700s in Kashmir, South Asia. Two forms are most easily used, however: mental rehearsal and mental imagery (a good third is hypnosis). The visualization technique may take one of three primary forms (sports examples follow):

- Mental rehearsal—seeing in your mind's eye a perfect movement, for example a stroke, shot, or turn;

- Mental imagery—imagining yourself as a powerful tool, as on a start imagining your legs as a powerful spring and the only thing that releases it is the starters signal, or imagine yourself as a fast animal, like a dolphin or a cheetah;

- Hypnosis—by someone such as the sports psychologist, hypnotherapist, or through self-hypnosis.

MENTAL REHEARSAL

Imagine in your mind's eye the perfect result actually coming true. See the actual incident or an experience of it happening. Use as many senses as possible, just as Lee Evans did prior to his world-record-setting 400-meter run at the Mexico City Olympics. Each day Lee imagined that he felt his foot plant for each stride, his lungs seeking more air, the crowd noise and colors, and so on. He used all of his senses in vivid imagination that he developed over the four previous years of training both physically and mentally.

Inwardly, see yourself at the site you wish to create for a perfect circumstance, movement, or competition. Notice the clothes you are wearing, the physical conditions (sounds, smells, temperature, and so on), and use *all* your senses. Feel yourself to be confident and relaxed. Visualize yourself completing a perfect performance from start to finish, and/or a particular skill or technique you wish to perfect. Imagine and feel it done perfectly with finesse, power, and confidence. Feel the complete experience that you visualize as if it is actually happening. Picture it so well that it is as if you are watching yourself with the best virtual reality device within your mind. The more vivid and detailed your *Winning Vision* is, the more readily the body and mind will respond with the perfect actions and thoughts. *Winning Vision* dramatically reduces any fears because you've already been there and done that!

MENTAL IMAGERY

Imagine that a part of your body is like a powerful tool, a fast animal, or the person you most wish to be. Be that which you imagine—feel its qualities of strength, speed, and character. A weightlifter may imagine her/himself to have the strength of an elephant, a sprinter that their legs are the most powerful spring and the starter's signal releases it, or the body of a gymnast is like that of a leaping Springbok/gazelle. Daily before practice or work, mentally see and feel your body and mind to have the qualities of the tool/person/animal.

VISION BOARD

You may also use your creative abilities by finding pictures in magazines that depict your perfect life's goal(s), or draw them. Attach these to a photo album, blank book, or poster paper on the wall of your room or office. Place an inspiring affirmation or quote that corresponds to the image above it. And each day look over the photos/drawings/affirmations and feel that they are yours today, that they are real. Imagine what it is like to reach your goal(s) as you view the images. To gain full value of the visualization practice, feel it throughout your body, know that it has happened already.

RESULTS

Frank Ryan, Ph.D., researched the value of combining visualization and the actual physical practice of an event. He divided up a physical education class into three equal sections. He tested them for free-throw percentage and then trained them for a month, an hour per day. The results were startling. Both Group 1 and Group 2 doubled their percentage while Group 3 *tripled* their accuracy!

- Group 1 did regular free-throw shooting practice.

- Group 2 simply imagined in their mind's eye making every free-throw.

- Group 3 practiced half visualization and half free throw shooting.

Try it for yourself! An author/friend of mine had been exposed to the idea of visualization and vision boards. He decided to give it a consistent try when exposed in the context of *Winning Ways*. He makes sure to visualize his ideal scene *each day*. As a result, and after several weeks of this, he commented, "I find the positive visualization seems to shove-aside my former cynicism, actually *replace* it, and these things I am evolving each day are actually in more motion now, coming true at a faster pace than before. I really believe I am now creating the life I want rather than always dealing with the life that otherwise happens to me. Wonderful! I wish I'd started the practice years and years ago, and I won't ever stop—In fact I really notice if I miss a day!"

GOALS

All the way back in 1953 a study showed that three percent of the Yale University graduating class had clearly stated, written goals. Twenty years later, this same three percent of the graduates had earned more than the other 97 percent who did not have written goals.

The Roman philosopher, Seneca, said, **"If a man does not know what port he is steering for, no wind is favorable to him."** You have to know where you are going in order to get there. This may seem simplistic, but many people have no idea where they are going in life. Some don't know where they are headed on the Journey of the Soul. Yet these are things that have to be *decided*, not simply *discovered*. Many people are waiting to discover what they should decide, to chance upon what they should be choosing. Are you one of them?

Goals are what you wish to achieve in the future—just as the goal of a marathon runner is to finish the 26 miles and 385 yards as fast as possible. You should have a specific "reachable" goal. *Life without a goal is like a race without a finish line.* Know where you are headed in your life. Set goals for yourself, your family, your school, your work, and your community. Your life will dramatically improve when you plan to achieve good goals. Create goals to improve the personal, social, academic, vocational, and spiritual aspects of your life.

THREE TYPES OF GOALS

There are three basic kinds of goals—short term, mid-term, and long-term:

- Short-term goals are to be met within three to six months. These are often called "objectives."

- Mid-term goals are to be achieved from six months to a year.

- Long-term goals are a year or longer.

SETTING GOALS

Start by setting some goals for yourself—choose from five to nine items that you wish to achieve in life—the quality of education you wish, the career you wish, the relationship you wish, and so on.

- At the top of a standard sheet of paper, list each one in a positive manner. Set as high a goal as you wish to put the necessary effort forth to achieve, and the reasons why you set them.

- Begin listing all the different ways and things you need to do to achieve each goal. These are called objectives. Be as specific as possible.

- Then each day, do the little actions that will bring about your goal(s).

And little actions make a big difference. As Helen Keller said:

"I long to accomplish a great and noble task. But it is my chief duty to accomplish humble tasks as though they were great and noble. The world is moving along, not only by the mighty shoves of its heroes but also by the aggregate of tiny pushes of each honest worker."

Here's an example of a well-stated goal:

- "I will lose 20 pounds in six months. I begin eating according to the *Virgin Diet.*

And here are a few examples of objectives:

- "I feel better by walking briskly at least a half an hour each night."

- "I enjoy drinking water and veggie drinks each day."

- "I happily share my activities with my buddy."

- "I feel stronger when I do push-ups and curl-ups daily to the best of my ability."

- "I am relieved when I ask for help or encouragement when I need it."

- "I feel great having earned an A-average this semester."

- "I feel proud that I ask questions when I don't fully understand."

Once you have set at least five goals with their five objectives each, read them over just before you go to sleep each night. This allows you to remember your plans and for your brain to ruminate over them while you sleep. You may wish to compile a success list to show that you are making progress each time you meet an objective or goal. Then evaluate what your next step or goal will be. Constantly reevaluate your goals and objectives, refining them and modifying them, growing into new challenges for growth to a more divine existence. After achieving a set number of goals/objectives, reward yourself with something special.

[4] CONCENTRATE

"The greatest athletes are legendary for their powers of concentration."

—MICHAEL MURPHY,

Founding Director, The Esalen Institute

IT'S THREE SECONDS LEFT in the championship game, and you can win it for your team—*if* you make two free throws. You have to concentrate *now*, with the whole yelling, waving crowd trying to distract you. Will you concentrate only on the shot? Do you have a trained mind able to focus at will? One of the areas often left out of sports training is concentration practice. I have heard coaches, teachers, and many parents say, "Concentrate on this! Concentrate now!" Yet I don't ever remember being taught *how* to concentrate. I can often concentrate when I'm asked, and at other times I cannot. Why? How can I learn to concentrate at will or on demand?

The founder of the Esalen Institute[5], Michael Murphy, wrote in *The Psychic Side of Sports*, "Every sport (and activity in life) requires concentration, freedom from distraction and sustained alertness. The development of athletic skill depends on one's ability to focus unbroken attention . . . A wandering mind diminishes ability . . . The greatest athletes are legendary for their powers of concentration." He is supported by Gail Roper (USA), who held 43 National Masters swimming records. She says, "You have to have a lot of mental power to win. It's like there's this energy out there and it's suspended in a mist or cobwebs. You have to collect that energy to win." We need to exercise the mind to focus at will on a chosen object or task, removing all distractions.

Daniel Goleman, the former Associate Editor of *Psychology Today* says, "When the mind gets focused, it reveals its inherent power which seems supernatural for ordinary people, even though it is natural." This is called *intense* concentration. Epitomizing this are the Lompong runners of Tibet, who bound over boulders and run up the Himalayan

---

[5] "The Esalen Institute, commonly just called Esalen, is an American retreat center and intentional community in Big Sur, California (specifically the community of Slates Hot Springs), which focuses upon humanistic alternative education.[2] Esalen is a nonprofit organization devoted to activities such as personal growth, meditation, massage, Gestalt Practice, yoga, psychology, ecology, spirituality, and organic food.[3] The institute offers more than 500 public workshops a year in addition to conferences, research initiatives, residential work-study programs, and internships." — https://en.wikipedia.org/wiki/Esalen_Institute

Mountains for hours. Day or night, they practice a super-concentration technique called (you guessed it) *meditation*.

Let's start with a few definitions. Concentration is paying attention to what you are doing in the moment, right where you are. "Concentration is a state of alertness, which makes it possible to focus my overall mental and physical activity on a specific object, person, or skill," says the noted German sports psychologist, Dr. Frank Schubert in his book, *Psychology from Start to Finish*. Archimedes, the Greek scholar, is said to have been so engrossed in his mathematical calculations that he was not aware of the invasion of the enemy forces in Syracuse. When shadows began to disturb his work, he turned around and asked the crowd to step to one side. He did not notice that the crowd was made up of enemy soldiers!

HOW TO CONCENTRATE

Let's start with two basic ways to concentrate before we delve into more intense practices and exercises. Simply put, to improve our concentration and thus our results, we need to *forget all else,* and we need to *become proficient.* Intuitive thinking is faster than the speed of thought. Like Archimedes, if we wish to reach our potential, we must be able to concentrate 100 percent on each task at hand. We must be aware of nothing else but what we are doing. You can do it in certain situations. **Forget everything that is not essential—by ignoring things, you are helping concentration. You begin investing in the causes for the consequences you desire, avoiding distractions and focusing the power of the mind on that which you wish to pursue. Thus we become the master of our mind and therefore, our**

actions. In fact it's an area (concentration) normally left out of a typical education!

Can we focus at will to remove the crowd noises and movements, to relax our breathing and shoot the hoops? Can we fully concentrate during a presentation to the board of directors? If your answers are "no," you should now continue reading and practice the following concentration methods.

If we try too hard to concentrate, we bring on internal stress and adversely affect our performance. We must, then, learn to bring concentration into our daily lives. Learning to become responsible for your own concentration is essential for peak performance. When you use imagery, tell yourself to be relaxed. Oral commands act as a support to the visual imagination. Concentration comes best when we are most interested in a subject or when we compete, and less when we do routine activities such as physical training and menial work.

A concentration technique should be easy to practice any time and all the time, not just in the heat of the moment. If you try to concentrate intensely it can have adverse effects, symptoms of anxiety, irregular breathing and heart rate, muscle tension, and more. But when you have a concentration technique that can be used regularly and easily each day, you won't have to try so hard. It will have become second nature. You will be able to use it without thinking. With consistent practice it will be easy.

Couple that focused attention with proficiency and your ability to concentrate will start to occur naturally and easily. Skiers spend many hours preparing and training for going down the slopes better and better. The elite skier trains year-round—intense dry land physical workouts during the off-season, or skiing in the Southern Hemisphere, and the constant zipping down the slopes, trails, and jumps when the snow blesses us with her presence. The casual skier may do some physical training prior to the first outing, and probably should do more in preparation. Yet what is missing from a skier's readiness? Are there ways to prevent injuries, enjoy the sport more, and improve at the same time?

Obviously, yes! According to studies done over the last 20 years, the elite skier is injured far less than the average skier. A primary reason given for this is that of concentration. On the average, an elite skier concentrates best, a Class 1 skier less, down to the casual skier, who concentrates least and is injured most. The elite skier has far fewer fears and doubts as compared to the other skiers. And according to Timothy Gallwey in his book *Inner Skiing:* "Fears and doubts are transferred to the body in the form of tensions, rigidity, and awkwardness preventing fluid movement." Thus making one susceptible to injury. The average and the elite skier alike report his or her most enjoyable time skiing, the times of peak performance, are as follows:

- You are physically free. Your body is able to move naturally, seemingly on its own, unhampered by tensions. You may even be surprised at your own strength, speed, or agility, even though there is no strain.

- You are mentally focused. Your attention is directed to the action, to the here-and-now. You are concerned with the activity and not thinking about the past or future.

- You are in harmony. No part of you conflicts with another—mind and body work together. You are moving with the action and have the feeling of being one with it.

- You are enjoying it. The experience is pleasurable, not just in terms of satisfaction with the results—it simply feels right. Skiers who are really involved frequently describe the peak performance in terms of its beauty.

Another aide to concentration is to understand that winning and losing are the opposite sides of the same coin. It is best to forget them both. We will then focus on the moment—the only area of our life which we have direct effect over. Concentration is important for living fully. When you lose your concentration, you are more apt to make a mistake. This mistake could lead to any number of negative experiences, if sometimes a positive one may come by chance.

Experiment with the following practices for better concentration, and observe the results in your performance and in your life. You'll be ready for the even more powerful concentration exercises that follow.

[5] CONCENTRATION EXERCISES

"When you relax your attention for a little, do not imagine
that you recover it whenever you wish."

—EPICTETUS, *Greek Stoic Philosopher*

PRACTICE #1

BEGIN TO BECOME aware of your breath throughout
your day. Become so conscious of it that you begin to hear it
in its normal rhythm. Stay focused on its ebb and flow, even
which nostril it enters and from which it leaves—this does
vary throughout the day. This exercise brings elementary
concentrated awareness.

PRACTICE #2

When you are sitting with nothing in particular to do, listen to the breath and pay attention to the space between breaths. The breath moves as a pendulum, pausing on each end. Concentrate on the space where the breath merges inside and emerges outside. Begin these first two practices now and for the next few weeks, as you read or go about your day. Concentration will begin to flow into your life at an accelerated rate to improve your every action.

PRACTICE #3

CUE WORD/MANTRA CONCENTRATION

The German philosopher, Meister Eckert once said, "A free mind has power to achieve all things." It may be unusual to remember your breath and let your mind go its merry way. We will bring deeper concentration by using a set of sounds to repeat with each breath. Over the past 40 years, I have used the syllables, HUM SO with great success. Psychologists call it a cue-word. The sun's rays focused by a magnifying glass can start a forest fire. Likewise, when the vibrations of the mind are on one chosen thought, we too have great power.

Mentally repeat HUM as you breathe in, and SO as you breathe out as you go about your day. HUM-SO is a powerful affirmation meaning, "I Am That," in the most ancient extant language in the world, Sanskrit. When possible, sit in a quiet room with your eyes closed and follow this practice for about 5-20 minutes each day for best results. This is the super concentration practice of meditation. When we focus our mind on HUM-SO with each breath, we begin to calm the breathing and brain waves, thus eliminating unnecessary thoughts of doubts, fears, and worry. We begin to think least, opening ourselves up to improved learning abilities, sports performance, and interpersonal relations. (Read the book *Superlearning*, by Ostrander and Schroeder for more on this.)

Bring concentration to yourself at will by practicing these first three techniques regularly during your day. When your peak performance is on the line, you'll more likely succeed.

PRACTICE #4

Simply follow the Golden Rule throughout your day: "Do unto others as you would have them do unto you." Keep the highest code of conduct as a person and you will have not only a clearer mind but improved performance and enhanced interpersonal relations, along with a good night's sleep.

PRACTICE #5

KARATE KID KONCENTRATION

Do you remember seeing the *Karate Kid* film series, the first movie and the second? This concentration technique combines breath with movement, as in "wax on, wax off." In the second film Daniel, the "Karate Kid," breaks blocks of ice with his hand. To accomplish this, he clasps his hands at his chest, fingers facing forward. As he breathes in, his hands move an arm's distance away parallel to the ground. As he breathes out the hands are returned to the chest. He then moves his arms upward high over the head as he breathes in. When the breath moves out, the arms move down to the starting position. He continues this rhythmic process of concentration for some time and then easily breaks the ice blocks. This technique brings the body and breath into harmony thus forcing the mind to follow suit. It is a very efficient method to use, once you are well practiced with it. Pretend you are "the kid" each night before going to bed. Practice this drill daily for three minutes, three times a day. You'll sleep better, too!

PRACTICE #6

OM NA-MAH SHI-VA-YA

Terry Ketchel, a fifth team guard for Duke University's football team, was told the mantra OM NA-MAH SHI-VA-YA over the telephone by his younger brother. Terry used it regularly, as much as he remembered—as instructed in Practice #3. Within six weeks, Terry was a starter on the team. He says, "My football was transformed. I was stronger and faster than ever before and could continue playing at the peak of effort—seemingly without effort. I just used the mantra a lot and felt great energy."

- Repeat OM NA-MAH SHI-VA-YA silently at your own rate of speaking, or

- While breathing in, mentally repeat OM NA-MAH SHI-VA-YA and while breathing out, repeat OM NA-MAH SHI-VA-YA.

- Listen to the mental repetition, hear each syllable, OM NA-MAH SHI-VA-YA, OM NA-MAH SHI-VA-YA, OM NA-MAH SHI-VA-YA, OM NA-MAH SHI-VA-YA, and the mind will become focused very quickly.

- Repeat it as often as possible—while sitting, standing, coming or going.

- Be aware of the meaning, "I honor my inner Self," as you repeat OM NA-MAH SHI-VA-YA.

This Self is the consciousness that motivates our thoughts and, therefore, our actions. When we repeat OM NA-MAH SHI-VA-YA, we tune into this force, concentrating our mental awareness on the source of our thoughts. We conserve amazing amounts of mental energy using OM NA-MAH SHI-VA-YA. This conserved and focused energy can then be used when we wish, giving us greater abilities in our daily lives.

Terry Ketchel became a lawyer and an assistant to a U.S. Senator, and he still uses the mantra! The practice of using a mantra as a cue word is an age-old practice. There are no books which deal with this technique and peak performance as yet (except this one). However, if you wish a deeper understanding of the uses and benefits of OM NA-MAH SHI-VA-YA, read *Journey to Joy* by Robert Shiarella, Ph.D.

PRACTICE #7

KI & AIKIDO

Professional baseball's career homerun world record holder, Sadaharu Oh (868 home runs in the Japanese league), learned and practiced another form of concentration, aikido, a Japanese martial art. One of the first things a student of aikido becomes aware of is his/her spirit center, located in the body about two fingers below the navel as described in the ki exercise. Aikido requires great balance and agility, both of which are possible only when you are perfectly centered. Sadaharu Oh had an unusual batting stance. He stood on one leg with the other cocked up, ready for the step forward. Upon learning of the "ki" or spirit center as it is called, Oh would practice hundreds of times to be conscious of the center while in his stance. He learned the way of spirit harmony, or aikido, and found that when he focused his energy in this center below the navel he had better balance, concentration, and power in his hitting.

Learn to focus your attention on the "ki" center in the lower abdomen now. Pay attention to the area two fingers below your navel. Feel your breath coming down into that center. Follow this awareness throughout your days. You will automatically see things better once your concentration is focused in this manner. Continue to do this focusing as you read. Simply become aware of the point below the navel. "Ki" is Japanese for "universal energy." In Chinese, it's called "Chi," and in English, it's the "Force." It can be applied when we are consciously focused on the spirit center two fingers below the navel.

A team of American baseball all-stars came through Japan and some players were interested in Sadaharu Oh's one-legged stance. Among them were Pete Pose, Rod Carew, Mike Schmidt, and "The Bull" Greg Luzinski. Arakawa-san, Oh's batting coach, got Luzinski to help him illustrate. He said, "I'll show you how Oh manages to bat on one foot. I will hold my arm horizontally; you try to bend it." Arakawa-san is just under 5'6" tall and had to look up to "The Bull."

"Are you sure? What will you do if I break your arm?" Luzinski asked.

Arakawa-san smiled and replied ever so softly, "Let's worry about that later. Try it. See what happens."

At first Luzinski was a little tentative with his strength. The arm did not move an inch. He smiled sheepishly, and said, "Well all right, here I go." He then tried with all his might. He turned red with the effort. Nothing! Arakawa-san's arm remained rigid and motionless. The foreign pressmen were very taken by this seeming feat of great strength. But it was not strength, it was the use of ki in a rather elementary way. Luzinski used strength, whereas Arakawa-san used *ki*. If you are doubtful, this is an exercise you may try yourself. No prior knowledge of aikido or ki is necessary:

KI EXERCISE

Do this with a friend or partner. Instruct the person to hold his or her arm out rigidly and with all their might, to resist your effort to bend their arm at the elbow. Unless this person is very, very much stronger than you,

you will succeed in bending their arm. Now instruct this partner to hold out their arm again, and instead of contracting the muscles in a pose of strength, have her or him imagine that power and light flows from the point just below their navel in a direct line to the shoulder and then through and beyond her or his arm, beaming outward from her or his fingertips through the wall of the room you are standing in. Make sure you instruct your partner to keep his or her hand open (rather than in a clinched fist) and to consciously forgo all thought of using any strength to resist you. The chances are that you will now have no more luck in bending your partner's arm than Luzinski did when he tried this with Arakawa-san.

The founder of aikido, Ueshiba Morihei, demonstrated this harmonious power one day in his dojo (training center). He took the long wood pole used in training for sword fighting and held it in the ready position raised in front of him. A student then took a baseball bat and hit the sword as hard as he could. Ueshiba's pole did not move at all with the impact. It was like hitting a concrete wall with the bat. This is the power of focused energy, the strength from achieving balance in the ki center. As Sadaharu Oh put it, "The goal of perfecting what was already in my own body seemed entirely natural."

PRACTICE #8

Magically Frozen

Let's pretend I'm a magician and I'm going to change all of you into an animal if I catch you. Once you are touched, you turn into stone—you cannot move from the position you were caught in, until the spell is broken. The one keeping the exact position when touched for that time period will break the spell and become the magician. Try your hand at this magic and make a task fun and with greater body control and mental concentration over longer periods of time.

PRACTICE #9

Moral concentration

Proper thoughts and actions play an important role in our ability to concentrate to improve our chances of winning. When we follow the Golden Rule—treating others as you would like to be treated, we have a clear conscience and focusable energy. If we are immoral, we worry about being caught. An athlete who uses steroids or other banned substances to improve his chances of winning, or an employee who steals from the company, or a manager who uses illegal aliens, and so on, they are all fearful of being caught. This wastes energy that could be channeled into improved performance. Life, and sports in particular, should uplift the morals and enjoyment of our society, setting a wonderful example for others.

PRACTICE #10

YANTRA/MANDALA

Using a visual focusing tool is powerful for many people. Try this: Simply gaze or focus on the white dot in the middle of this image. It is an ancient symbol of creation. It is called, Sri Yantra or Sri Chakra in Sanskrit.

PRACTICE #11

CHARTRES LABYRINTH

Image:
https://upload.wikimedia.org/wikipedia/commons/thumb/3/35/Labyrinthus.svg/
1024px-Labyrinthus.svg.png

Labyrinths are found around the world and were first created in prehistoric times. A story with a labyrinth is most often remembered from the ancient Greek legend of Theseus and the Minotaur. However, true labyrinths have no false pathways, as do mazes. Labyrinths are also said to be physical images of the twists and turns in our path in life itself. Labyrinths have been seen on stone and wood-carvings, painted on walls or in artwork, woven into blankets or baskets or fabrics, laid out in stone on the ground or in a church, cut into the turf, or grown with hedges.

Labyrinths provide a test of skill for the eye or the feet to follow, and an exercise for the mind and the body. While traversing the labyrinth one may choose to find out what is happening within oneself. Notice the feelings and thoughts, the visions and impressions that come up while moving through the labyrinth. Labyrinths have been used for many reasons throughout history. They have been used as a dancing ground and as ceremonial pathways.

For concentration purposes use a pen or pencil on the image to trace the path in from the entrance, pause, then retrace back out. If you have a full-sized image on the ground, walk it calmly as you focus on the breath with each step. Upon reaching the center, pause at any or all petals or in the center, then retrace your steps out. Labyrinths may be used for agility drills, trust walks, and so many other useful experiences. You may wish to visit www.labyrinthsociety.org.

SUMMARY

There are many more forms of concentration techniques. Try some of these for several weeks and see the positive results flow into your life. If you want even more tricks you could read the many books on focusing and centering concentration available on the market, but this may have the reverse effect because you begin to water down your energy by spreading it out amongst too many techniques. To avoid this, practice three of your favorite methods diligently for six weeks. You won't then need any others.

"This is so profound, because you have the potential—

and I see the potential in you.

You don't see the potential you have.

I want you to transform."

—PREM RAWAT, AMAROO, 9/19/16

BOOK TWO ~ BODY

"In the end, it's extra effort that separates a winner from second place. But winning takes a lot more than that, too. It starts with complete command of the fundamentals. Then it takes desire, determination, discipline, and self-sacrifice. And finally, it takes a great deal of love, fairness and respect for your fellow man. Put all these together, and even if you don't win, how can you lose?"

—Jesse Owens

[6] BREATHE

"The Lord formed man out of clay of the ground and blew
into his nostrils the breath of life, and so man became a living
being."

—THE BOOK OF GENESIS 2:7

AH, THE BREATH OF LIFE! What a topic and yet seldom,
if ever explored or experimented with by people in their
entire life. Yet there is a science, thousands-of-years-old, from
Asia, called Pranayama[6], it prompts numerous and diverse
benefits. Just learn a few practices and you can be healthier,

---

[6] "Pranayama is control of Breath". "Prana" is Breath or vital energy
in the body. On subtle levels prana represents the pranic energy
responsible for life or life force, and "ayama" means control. So
Pranayama   is   "Control   of   Breath".   —
www.yogapoint.com/info/pranayama.htm

happier, and according to some, holier! I personally knew an 80-plus-year-old Indian music master, Swami Nadabrahamananda, who was tested at the Neuro-Psychiatric Institute (NPI) at the University of California, Los Angeles (UCLA). They encased him in a transparent air-tight container. When the candle went out, the timer started as he played his tablas[7] with two images of his chosen deity (Shiva) to see. He then practiced a form of Pranayama called Kumbakah, or breath retention—not forcefully, but simply *allowing* the retention of the breath. During the 30 minutes of "airless confinement," he was checked for vital signs. He was then released unscathed by what most considered an ordeal— one he took so nonchalantly. He simply and calmly *allowed* the breath to stay inside during his state of active meditation.

The breath is vitally important in our life. Yet, the respiratory+ system is one of the least trained and consciously developed areas of the body with its great influence on the mind. The average adult breathes 26,000 times a day—a child even more. This provides oxygen for the body, especially the brain. Proper breathing brings subtle and yet powerful energy for enthusiastic, concentrated actions. The mind is also cleared of extraneous thoughts with optimum breathing practices. The German philosopher, Meister Eckert once said, "A free mind has power to achieve all things." Is that a worthy goal?

How many people practice holding their breath for extended periods of time? We did it as youthful swimmers at home. How many laps could we do underwater? Learning

---

[7] The tabla is a membranophone percussion instrument, which is often used in Hindustani classical music and in the traditional music of Afghanistan, India, Pakistan, Nepal, Bangladesh, and Sri Lanka. — Wikipedia

more about physiology as I grew older and studied the field of performance, I found that the lungs may expand more through this regular practice, thus holding more oxygen. For example, a man ran 17 miles at a six-minute-mile pace throughout. His average heart beat-per-minute (BPM) was never over 130. He had practiced breath training for just 18 months.

When the ribs are elastic-like and moving fully with each breath, the massage they provide helps maintain a flexible and young body and mind. Nasal breathing filters the air of impurities with the mucous membrane, also preventing infections. Breathing through the nose also regulates the temperature and humidity in the air entering the bronchioles and lungs. Breathing through the nose brings oxygen to the lower lobes of the lungs where most of the air-sacs are. This stimulates optimum absorption of oxygen into the bloodstream. As the wind drives smoke and impurities away, breath training removes impurities and brings clarity and strength to the body and mind.

BREATH TRAINING

CONCENTRATED BREATHING

- Do breath training through the nose as much as possible.

- Exhale completely to begin.

- Use the diaphragm—it ensures the filling of the lower lobes of the lungs, where the majority of the oxygen exchange takes place.

- Draw the breath in using the diaphragm by expanding the abdomen then expand the chest to completely fill the lungs.

- Do the breath training exactly as instructed.

- Do breath training to your own capacity—do not exceed it!

CATCH YOUR BREATH

Begin to become aware of your breath—which nostril it enters and leaves. As described, use the diaphragm to bring the air through the nose to the lower lobes of the lungs, the ribs expand to fill the middle, and the upper chest and shoulders to top them off with energizing oxygen. Stay focused on the ebb and flow of your breathing. Pay attention to the space *between* the breath. Concentrate on the space where the breath merges inside and where it emerges outside. Feel the stream of oxygen fill the bottom of the lungs up to the top, just as a glass is filled with sweet, energetic mango juice. This builds a foundation for concentrated awareness to improve your every action.

DARTH VADER BREATHING

During exercise use this technique. Breathe through the nose, while making the sound of Darth Vader, especially on the exhalation. Practice at your own rate and remain relaxed throughout your training. To breathe as Darth Vader does:

- Constrict the throat slightly with each breath.

- While exhaling use the diaphragm by constricting the abdomen and feel the air move to the top of your head.

- As you inhale, feel the breath move all the way to the rear of the head and throat and then into your lungs.

Darth Vader Breathing (DVB) will help bring endurance and strength to the body, while calming the mind, and increasing will power. Bring concentration to yourself at will by practicing DVB regularly during your day. Because you integrate this practice more into your daily life, you'll more likely succeed when your peak performance is needed.

BHASTRIKA

Bhastrika (the Breath of Fire) is an extremely powerful, sensitive, and important practice. It is said to eliminate diseases, especially those of the stomach. Bhastrika also tones the muscles of the stomach, so a fat stomach becomes flatter. Bhastrika demands that you be strong and disciplined. You should be regular in your practice. Do it as perfectly as possible—when you practice this technique, you shouldn't make the tiniest mistake.

To practice Bhastrika, sit in the full lotus position (called "padmasana") or a posture where both knees touch the floor. The spine must be straight, with the shoulders level, and the hands resting on the knees with the forefinger and thumb touching and the other fingers out straight (in the chin mudra[8]) while the arms remain straight. The posture must remain constantly straight and steady without tension or stiffness. Become focused by using the mantra or focusing on the Force within.

Image: lotus position
https://upload.wikimedia.org/wikipedia/commons/a/af/Lotus_position.svg

---

[8] A mudra (i/muˈdrɑː/; Sanskrit mudrā, "seal", "mark", or "gesture"; Tibetan: ཕྱག་རྒྱ་ THL chakgya) is a symbolic or ritual gesture in Hinduism and Buddhism. While some mudras involve the entire body, most are performed with the hands and fingers. —Wikipedia

When a child is born its first breath is an exhalation. Bhastrika also begins with the exhalation. First, breathe out through the nostrils with great force, then continue breathing in and out with a lot of strength, as long as you don't get exhausted. Focus primarily on the exhalation as the in-breath will naturally occur because nature abhors a vacuum. When you have reached your limit of comfort, then breathe in completely. Hold the breath as long as you comfortably can, then take in a little more air before exhaling slowly.

During the time when the breath is retained, close off the two main exits of energy (called Bandhas) by bending your chin down toward the chest while contracting the anal sphincter (between the anus and genitals). At the end of comfortable retention, release these before taking in a little more oxygen and then exhale slowly and completely. *Remain relaxed during Bhastrika.* After practicing Bhastrika sit quietly in meditation for five minutes, then lie down in the corpse/death pose (shavasana) for five more minutes to completely still the mind and absorb the energy throughout your body.

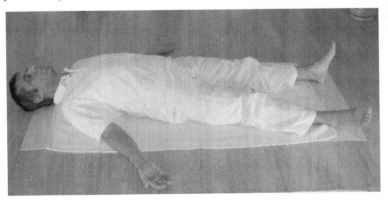

Image: shavasana or mrtasana (death pose)

https://upload.wikimedia.org/wikipedia/commons/9/9f/Shavasana.jpg

In the beginning, you may find it difficult to do, but as you continue the practice, you will start enjoying it. After a week, do two rounds, after two weeks do three Bhastrikas, and after a month you can do four rounds. Women can have a five-day vacation each month from Bhastrika (through their menstrual cycle). Don't eat two hours before nor one hour after practicing Bhastrika, and you should never do Bhastrika before or after over-eating.

[7] What Meditation Is and Does

"The soul should concentrate itself by itself."

—Plato

HISTORICALLY, MEDITATION IS having one chosen thought in your mind for a long period of time. This long period of time is *not* one minute—not the one-to-ten-second segments of TV or movie images flashing at you. Sounds daunting, eh? It isn't. Just like the journey of 1,000 miles or learning to walk, your ability to win from meditation simply evolves one step at a time, one sitting (or lying or walking) at a time. According to Patanjali, the scholar who codified yoga in the second century, B.C: "Meditation is the uninterrupted flow of concentration toward an object." In other words, meditation is super concentration, and the importance of concentration is obvious for anything. The greatest thinkers, creative artists, and athletes are legendary for their powers of concentration.

We talked about Bob Beamon, who spontaneously got into a meditative state in his long jump competition at the Mexico City Olympics in 1968. While most records are broken by a fraction of an inch, Bob leapt nearly two feet further than anyone in history. He became a sport psychologist to learn how to consciously, at will, get into that state of bliss and peak performance. I met him after his keynote presentation at the 1984 Olympic Scientific Congress's Sport Psychology section. We talked about this very topic, as my presentation was titled, "Meditation and the Ultimate Performance in Sports."

WHAT MEDITATION DOES

"The mind is sharper and keener in seclusion and uninterrupted solitude. Be alone—that is the secret of invention; be alone, that is when ideas are born."

—NIKOLA TESLA

Throughout the ages in all cultures and traditions, people have learned methods for contacting or accessing the powers of the spirit—from shamans, priests, gurus, holy people, or transpersonal psychologists. Most of the practices taught by these extraordinary people calmed the mind down from its incessant chatter. If our mind is off during a competition or other activity because of fear or anger or other reason, no matter how well trained we are, our performance suffers.

One of the most effective methods to bring our mind into our control is meditation. It eliminates psychological barriers while developing willpower. It brings speedy relaxation, manages stress, replenishes energy, and opens energy channels. Joseph Chilton Pearce, the noted human developmentalist, states in his book *The Bond of Power*, "Meditation trains thought to be one-pointed in the face of the brain's continual barrage of sensory impressions and desires." Meditation is said to be the state of mind where all optimum performance occurs, as it accesses our inherent spirit. Research indicates that it improves academics and business and work efficiency through improved concentration and better attendance because you're healthier, it reduces respiratory ailments, it improves cardio-vascular efficiency, and so much more. Christopher Magarey, M.D., a noted Australian cancer physician, indicates that, "Meditation can help turn your attention inwards, drawing on untapped energy, thus reducing the negativity of trauma (stress)." And one of the most famous modern stress researchers, Kenneth Pellitier, found that meditation gives relaxation between stress periods. The calm, relaxed mind that comes with meditation in turn calms and relaxes the body.

Meditation stills the mind to experience its source. It acts to purge past conditionings and impressions in the sub-conscious mind. Meditation opens up the mind allowing it to be unencumbered by weighty negativities. Historically, peace of mind is accomplished through meditation. It calms the mind from the savage waters of uncontrolled thought. It brings peace to your inner and your outer world. Meditation breaks down psychological barriers comprised of fears and doubts. It opens a channel internally to clear out our addictive behavior and character defects. **"Meditation is extremely useful in treating anxiety attacks, it lowers blood pressure, can ease circulatory problems, and migraine and tension headaches,"** says Herbert Benson, M.D., Harvard University Cardiologist

Health is improved, especially when combined with affirmations/afformations and visualization techniques. Interpersonal relations are enhanced with the improved self-image brought on by meditation as indicated in Joseph C. Pearce's work *The Magical Child Matures*. Self-realization or attunement with the divine or universal power is attained through dedicated practice of meditation as witnessed and illustrated by people in all the scriptures of the world.

Martial arts teach how to focus spiritual energy, called "ki," and intensify it through meditation. An interesting experiment by Khalsa in her 1983 master's thesis illustrated that the "ki" goes wherever your attention goes, and meditation helps us to focus this conscious energy. Meditation opens energy channels. It clears the brain of unnecessary activity. When the brain is calm we are calm, and we can produce better. We have a clearer view of any activity. In *The Centered Athlete*, Gay Hendricks says, "The highly-skilled professional is able to get his mind out of the way, so thinking isn't necessary—only acting in well-trained ways. Thinking takes too much time." Creative inspiration occurs when the mind is calm. Einstein, was inspired with $E=MC^2$ while sailing. Isaac Newton arrived at the Law of Gravity while relaxing in a meditative state of mind under a tree in serene nature.

Lactic acid, a symptom of fatigue, is removed from the body by only 20 minutes of meditation, twice a day, in fact, it takes eight hours of sleep to remove as much lactic acid as the meditation practice. It thereby rejuvenates the bodily energy. It is said to bring the state of mind necessary for all peak performances. Let's summarize some of the uses or benefits of meditation:

- Health

- Stress reduction

- Releases anxiety

- Prompts relaxation

- Revitalizes bodily and mental energies

- Promotes happiness

- Decreases depression

- Learning (studies show one grade point higher!)

- Self Improvement

- Being intimate with reality—unencumbered by mental and sociological conditions

- Creativity—opens one to creative sources within!

- Peacemaking—fewer classroom disruptions, cease fires, less violence/crime

- Peak performance and optimum health.

Let's expand on some very significant benefits of meditation—willpower, focus, and awareness of awareness:

WILLPOWER

Meditation develops the will—the ability and desire to hold to one-pointedness and discrimination in the face of confusion and distractions. Increased will power through meditation can improve both performance and enjoyment in sports because it brings us to a deeper center, a truer and more effective level of personal functioning. This center within is often called the "inner Self." It is pure consciousness, the source of our intellect, intuition, enthusiasm, energy, inspiration, and more. Extraordinary feats often result when people tap the powers of the Self by having a calm mind. For example, when threatened by fire, people often display powers that they would never dream of in ordinary life. People of all sizes and shapes have been known to lift automobiles and to drag children out from under them.

FOCUS

Meditation eliminates psychological barriers. A young high jumper did not think he could go over 210 centimeters (6'9"), as his best was just 203 cm (6'6"). This was his psychological barrier. In less than three months of meditation and practice, he leapt 216 cm (7'1"). When describing the jump to me later, he gave a clear explanation of just why meditation works for improving performance. When I asked him what it was like going over the bar, he paused for a moment, trying to remember. Finally he said, "I don't know. The first thing I remember is looking up at the bar from the pit." This is a description of a mental state totally free from thought, a state so deep that his attention was freed from all outside pulls so that he was able to channel all his energy into the jump. All the psychological barriers we usually experience in our lives, all the self-imposed mental limitations which prevent full expression of our potential are eliminated in this state of deep meditation.

AWARENESS OF AWARENESS

And meditation puts us in touch with the witness of the mind. This Self or "witness" watches our lives unfold while we are awake, witnesses the dreams in the mind, and is aware that we have experienced a deep sleep. William Glasser, M.D. says that "Physiologically, the meditator quickly gains more access to the brain, an access not usually achieved by most of us who never take this regular time."

[8] MEDITATE!

"God dwells within you as you. See God in each other."

—MUKTANANDA PARAMHANSA

PREPARATIONS FOR MEDITATION

Preparations for meditating include:

- Asan—a wool or silk cloth, cushion, mat, or chair to sit upon;

- An intention for reaching the depth of a calm mind or another profound intention (for you).

And the following are not necessary but helpful as proven by millions of people for thousands of years:

- Incense or essential oil to add a pleasant calming fragrance;

- A lit candle;

- A photo or statue of a personal inspiration, or a spiritual or religious image;

- Clothes worn particularly for meditation;

- Being directly on the Earth either on the wool or silk Asana or directly on Mother Earth to receive the calming vibrations to bring every cell into harmonious synchronistic balance;

- Open airflow—if conducive for concentration and comfort.

A SIMPLE MEDITATION

Start simple. Meditation may be done while sitting, walking, standing or lying down—it just depends on which suits you most. The majority of people who learn and practice meditation sit erect, either in a chair or on the floor or ground. And ultimately, you will be able to be in a state of meditation *all* of the time!

Initially, this first technique should be done in a quiet room. Sit in a comfortable, erect position with your eyes closed. Invoke God to "Please bless this activity," or tell your mind, "It's peacetime." It may be difficult to remember your breath at first because your mind is used to going its own way, so we'll avoid this problem and bring deeper concentration by using a set of sounds to repeat with each breath. As mentioned, I have used with great success the syllables HUM-SO. Mentally repeat HUM as you breathe in, and SO as you breathe out (you can actually do this as you go about your day, also). When we focus our mind on HUM-SO with each breath, we begin to calm the breathing and brain waves, thus eliminating unnecessary thoughts of doubts, fears, and worry. We begin to think least, opening ourselves up to improved learning abilities, sports performance, and interpersonal relations. So set aside 10 to 30 minutes each day upon awakening and/or before going to sleep to perform this simple meditation:

- Sit in a comfortable upright position with the eyes closed and focus on the breath coming in HUM and out with SO, or you may simply repeat the word "Love."

- Pay attention to the space between the breaths, where the breath merges inside and emerges outside. It is a space of peace and tranquility. This calm space between the moving breath is the source of your breath and thoughts.

- If any thoughts come to mind simply return to listening to the breath move in with HUM and out with SO.

- This practice trains your mind to be in your control, so when you need it calm and focused in the game-winning situation, you have it.

- Meditate for about 20 to 60 minutes once or twice each day. Honor yourself with a strict self-discipline for this valuable activity.

This technique takes the mind away from distractions of fear, competitors, fatigue, and other inhibitors to peak performance. The mind's energy is focused and the body can then do what it has been trained for. It then naturally does well and moves fluidly. It will also stabilize you for more wonderful and efficient days. Soon your mind will become so focused that the sound, the breath, and thoughts will disappear, giving us an opportunity to experience true peace of mind. In this state of brainwave activity, we are open to creative inspiration, we are in a peak experience and performance state of mind, all while experiencing a deep state of relaxation. It is optimum to practice meditation a few minutes prior to each visualization or anything that is very important. If you have a profound experience during meditation, consult a master of this art or read *Play of Consciousness* by Baba Muktananda for greater understanding, and progress into deeper states of meditation.

MORE FORMS OF MEDITATION

There are many forms of meditation. The most common ones use a cue-word or mantra, a harmonious set of syllables with a profound meaning. We can learn one that uses cue-words with the simple practice of attention on the breath. This enables us to get into concentration very quickly. The added understanding of the meaning of the mantra actually "programs" the unconscious to accept the truth. The breath begins to slow when we allow the mind to calm down. The heartbeat and brainwaves follow suit and also calm down. In this manner we gain speedy relaxation and control over the mind and therefore, it's control over the body. Some forms of meditation include:

- Buddhist/Vipassana/Mindfulness;

- Yogi/Mantra meditation—powerful cue words for concentration/meditation;

- Siddha—Shaktipat, Kundalini awakening of meditative energy;

- Zen and/or labyrinth (Chartres) walking;

- Mandala—Sri Yantra, Tibetan, or other focusing images;

- Guided meditation—visualization;

- Tratak—focus on flame of candle;

- Gong—focus on the flowing sound;

- Laughing—lets the thoughts release and the lightheartedness begin!

[9] WARM-UP & COOL-DOWN

"If you don't take care of your body where will you live?"

—ANONYMOUS

WE'VE SHARPENED OUR MINDS to this point, and learned the *Winning Way* of conscious breathing. Let's focus on the body a little more, as we balance our approach to body, mind, and spirit. The purpose of warm-ups and cool-downs are to prompt the body for peak performance and health. With these *Winning Ways* practices, the cardiovascular, respiratory, and endocrine systems are stimulated. The body is stretched, thus preventing stress-related stiffness or injuries and the accumulation of lactic acid in the muscles.

After a day of work or intense training or competition, one must cool down and mellow out properly by stretching and relaxing the muscles. This releases stress, stimulates the brain, enables efficient movement and effective training or competition when done properly. In his book, *Holistic Medicine*, Dr. Kenneth Pelletier, M. D., writes about these particular techniques as "both strengthening and lengthening muscles while reducing stress." Many athletes, coaches and fitness buffs consider warming up and cooling down time-consuming nuisances and frequently avoid them, but static stretching before *and* after a workout or competition is one of the most important elements of an effective conditioning program. Most fitness experts insist that if you don't have time to warm up and cool down, you don't have time to train.

To increase blood flow to the muscles, it is good to do some light jogging or aerobic exercise for a few minutes before beginning your warm-ups. The proper breathing combined with stretching forces oxygenated blood deep into the fibers of the muscles for an exhilarating effect. Fifteen minutes of warm-ups and cool-downs will elongate the muscles, and with the increased blood flow they become supple and better prepared for a good workout. The stretches should be done to your rate and ability. Never overstretch, as this may cause damage to muscles or connective tissues. Move into a position and feel *pressure*—not pain. Breathe in completely through the nose and out through the mouth. This breathing practice filters the air through the nose, warming it to body temperature before it comes into the lungs.

Set up a basic routine that may be enhanced when necessary for work on a particular area of need. The full-body should be stimulated from the front and back to each side and the internal organs as well. This is the reason for our using Hatha Yoga as the preparation and culmination of our training sessions. Hatha Yoga has been proven to work on the whole body, the major and minor muscle structure, and each bodily system is toned or stimulated while the mind is able to focus and become prepared for peak performance. With the proper warm-ups prior to, and effective cool-downs after a training or competition, there are many benefits, as we:

- Bring the breathing into stimulated balance;

- Remove toxins like lactic acid from the muscles and blood;

- Oxygenate the system;

- Stretch the muscles to remove tensions and improve or retain flexibility;

- Prepare ourselves for the day's experiences, training/competition;

- Prevent injuries by stretching the muscles, stimulating the joints full movement, and toning the connective tissue;

- Stimulate the endocrine system to balance the production of hormones for the upcoming activity;

- Energize the internal organs;

- Synchronize the body/mind/spirit;

- Spur the mind to concentrate on our chosen topic/training/competition;

- Stretch the mental limitation.

The warm-up and cool-down phase of training is a must and should be done in a complete manner. Many people just do stretching on some of the major muscles used in the exercise. This ignores the many muscles, connective tissue, and internal organs that need to be brought into a balance and tone for the stresses imposed upon them during training, competition, or the workday. The prevention of injuries is best done with a simple practice of warm-ups and cool-downs, combined with also following proper mental and physical training schedules. Cooling down helps prevent pulled muscles and torn tendons. Cooling down is the most neglected, underused, or misused practice on a person's training schedule. In fact, the necessity for stretching the body after a training has been emphasized at all the Olympic Scientific Congresses since 1984.

As with warm-ups, the cool-down phase of training is a must and should be done in a complete manner. During strenuous activity, lactic acid—a waste product of anaerobic exercise—builds up in muscle tissues causing aching and fatigue. Muscles in this condition continue to contract, which is a sign that they are still working. Proper stretching with the breath after training will remove much of this byproduct of training. This will cause the muscles to relax and recover more quickly, allowing for more efficient use of training time, and helps to prevent injuries.

The most dramatic example of the need for properly cooling down is illustrated by a great proponent of this process, Al Oerter. Al was a gold medal winner in the discus during four successive Olympics. Al was attempting to go for a fifth, when in a preliminary track meet, just prior to the American Olympic trials, at San Jose State University, Al injured himself. He was simply walking away from the ring after a throw and his Achilles tendon snapped. Relating why this happened, Al said that for two days he had performed intense strength practices and did not cool down enough after them. This led him to be stiffer than normal and the tight muscles finally forced the tendon to snap from the bone. As Al normally cooled down after each training, he knew this was necessary for better performance, and now he knows, and so do you, that it is best to properly cool down after all trainings and competitions.

After a day of work, or training or competition, we let our breathing return to normal naturally, then we begin the cool-downs. They are done at a regular rate to begin with and we then calm them down as you progress, as your breathing calms down. If one side of your body is less supple than the other, spend twice as long in each posture which stretches that side.

The "S.S. Stretch" (see below) is an excellent and highly recommended warm-up and cool-down. These exercises need to include the properties of toning and strengthening the body, focusing the mind, and opening a person to the Force/energy. There have been many such exercises developed in the Orient along with the many forms of martial arts, from aikido to taekwondo. If you had to choose only one exercise to do on a daily basis for health and fitness, this has the most benefit and can be done without anything special and in confined quarters (God forbid).

SUN SALUTATION STRETCH

The "S.S. Stretch"

A simple and effective practice for fitness and/or warming up or cooling down is the Sun Salutation or "SS Stretch" of Hatha Yoga. It can be done at an aerobic or anaerobic rate. It tones and stretches the muscles, thus preventing injury; it stimulates the internal organs; it refines the functioning of the glands; it focuses the mind and opens oneself to the spirit— all this while promoting health and stimulating the effective flow of energy within the body. It prepares us for physical exertion and loosens every part of the body. Our breathing capacity is developed, while the spine becomes flexible and strong. The various movements stimulate the entire body, including all the systems, especially the endocrine, circulatory, respiratory, and digestive. The gentle stretching greatly assists in loosening the joints and muscles of the legs and back. The synchronization of the movements and the balanced rhythm of the breath develops coordination and breath control. It is also a great eye exercise.

The SS Stretch can be used as a workout when done rapidly for 20 minutes, or as preparation and/or culmination of a training/competition session, when done slowly. As a warm-up, begin the SS Stretch slowly, increasing the speed while doing 7 to 12 repetitions. As a cool-down, begin as fast as the breath moves, slowing down as you do at least seven repetitions. Focus on letting tensions go while stretching to feel pressure, not pain. Only breathe through the nose, unless this is impossible. Breathe in while bending backward; breathe out while bending forward. *Follow the instructions exactly, and again, do the stretch at your own ability level.*

1. Stand up straight with the feet comfortably shoulder-width apart. FOCUS YOUR MIND ON YOUR BREATH. Palms touching, at the middle of your chest, fingers pointing upward. EXHALE COMPLETELY.

2. As you BREATHE IN, raise the arms over the head, locking the thumbs, while keeping the arms alongside the ears. Bend backward, as the hips move forward, look up and back into your head.

3. Keeping the head between the arms while bending forward, BREATHE OUT bringing the hands on each side of the feet/legs. The knees are kept straight. Try to gently bring the face to the knees.

4. Keep the left foot between the hands, stretch the right leg back with the knee to the floor. BREATHE IN lifting the shoulders up and tilt the head backwards as you look up and back into your head.

5. Bring the left foot back even with the right foot. BREATHE OUT while lifting the hips high forming a triangle. The head between the arms and, if possible, the heels touching the floor. Look at the feet. Try to look down at your cheeks.

6. In succession, bring the knees, chest, and chin to the floor. The hips (pelvis) should be kept raised from the floor. The palms are now beneath the shoulders. RETAIN THE BREATH.

7. Drop the pelvis to the floor while BREATHING IN as you tighten the buttocks, raising the head

backward, neck and chest up, and look backward into the head. The elbows remain alongside the body, slightly bent so that the pressure is distributed along the whole back.

8. In one motion, EXHALING, lift the hips high, bringing the head between the arms, and look down at your cheeks. Heels toward the floor forming a triangle. (Same as #5.)

9. As you BREATH OUT, thrust the right foot forward between the hands, with the knee up in the chest area. The left knee remains stretched back touching the floor. (Similar to #4, legs reversed.)

10. EXHALING, bring the left foot forward next to the other, straighten the knees. Place the palms flat alongside the feet. Bring the face to the knees while looking down at your cheeks (it's a wonderful eye exercise). (Same as #3.)

11. Keeping the arms alongside the ears, lock the thumbs together and INHALE while stretching up and bending backward. Look up and back into your head. (Same as #2.)

12. EXHALING, return to the beginning position, hands at the chest, palms together, stand erect. (Same as #1.)

This is half a round. Repeat the instructions with the opposite leg for a complete round. Do a minimum of 7 to 12 rounds a day—no need to do more than 100 rounds. Refer for more details to Dyananda, S., *Hatha Yoga for Meditators* (S. Fallsburg, NY: SYDA Foundation).

Other specific postures of Hatha Yoga may be practiced for various sports or a simple fitness regime. There are innumerable research articles about the effects of yoga for fitness and performance published in the *SNIPES Journal* at the National Institute of Sports, Patiala, India.

[10] GET NOURISHED

"God gave you every plant yielding seed and trees bearing
fruit as your food, and animals as your domain."

—GENESIS 1:29

SINCE 1973, I HAVE ADJUSTED MY DIET to fresh,
whole unadulterated foods. Initially, I lost 20 excess pounds.
Psychologically, I felt and acted lighter. I had more energy to
go through my long day of teaching at the inner-city high
school and teaching night courses in yoga at a local
community college. During this time I was waking up at 3
a.m. to meditate and work around my home before going to
teach, and I was going to bed at 11 p.m. each night. Knowing
an optimum diet would give me more energy and strength, I
researched and discovered that such a diet would also

improve I.Q. and endurance. Dr. Michael Colgan, Ph.D., who gave the sports nutrition keynote speech at the 1984 Olympic Scientific Congress, (the most prestigious Sports Sciences Conference in the world, held along with the Summer Olympics) found that I.Q. could be improved up to 20 points, and endurance and strength up to 50 percent with proper nutritional supplementation.

This confirmed my assumptions and research. Nutrition can affect the mind in positive or negative ways. The neuro-endocrinologist, R. Wurtman, showed in a study that complex-carbohydrates can have the same effect on people as anti-depressant drugs. They can improve mood, diminish sensitivity to negative stimuli, and ease the way to sleep.

The spirit is affected by and can affect food, so be silent or pray a bit prior to eating. Oriental research over the centuries, verified by modern science, has shown that the best food for the body, mind, and spirit is that which is fresh, whole, unadulterated, and as live as possible. "Live" vegetables offer a person more highly oxygenated food with an ability to oxygenate their system. It should be grown naturally, without chemicals. The optimum is not just organic but "biodynamic!"

In fact, air, liquids, food, and thoughts are the nourishing forces for humans. The purest and freshest forms of nourishment should be used for peak performance. The best foods are those that keep the body healthy, elevate the mind, and free the spirit. The amount of nutrients, as well as when and how they are ingested, can be nearly as important as what is ingested.

Looking at average swim training programs at the beginning of the 20th century, they consisted of about one hour of physical exercises, no mental or spirit training, no diet restrictions, and little distance work. By the later parts of the century, we have four to eight times the hours for training sessions and up to 16 times the meters swum per day. Mental training is now a part of the elite athletes regimen, and everyone is very aware of their dietary habits.

The way things are going, then, evolving into the 21st century, we will have less hours of physical training, thus preventing early burn-out, with more time spent in mental and metaphysical exercises, and many people are eating less red meat while many of the elite athletes are eating less meat of any kind, with more fresh, live, whole, and organic foods. The performances are awesome compared to those of the previous ten years. In fact, dramatic examples of the value of proper nutrition are described by Colgan (1982), who keynoted the 1984 Olympic Scientific Congress' Sports Nutrition section, and observed improved marathon times of up to 28 minutes with an average of over 11 minutes, only about six minutes for the control group.

"One cannot think well, love well, sleep well, if one has not dined well."

—VIRGINIA WOOLF

PURE FOODS

Generally speaking, pure, fresh, wholesome foods, low in complex carbohydrates and moderate in proteins and high quality fats are best. This has been proven by centuries of use and recently verified by modern science. However, some soils may lack proper nutrients and the preparation of foods may destroy other nutrients thus necessitating proper supplementation. How much and which vitamins and minerals are needed? This is truly an individual exigency. A qualified nutritionist should be consulted for fine-tuning the body's nutrient needs. Should this not be possible, use applied kinesiology[9] (see the book, *Your Body Doesn't Lie* by Dr. John Diamond) or a chiropractic doctor.

Pure foods are those having no additives, such as colorings, flavorings, preservatives, and so on. Many of the colorings found in soft drinks and ketchup, for example, are *carcinogenic*—they cause cancer or clog the body in an unfavorable manner. Most processed meats contain deliberately added hormones for speedy growth (more money faster), nitrates as preservatives, and color enhancers to make it look fresher than it is. These additives may form carcinogenic material, both in cooking and/or in the interaction with digestive juices. Whereas preservatives do just that—preserve in our system and therefore clog the smooth functioning of the body.

WATER

The universal nutrient is pure water. It is an imperative. Hass (1983) and Diamond (1985) explained that every chemical reaction in the body, including energy production, takes place in a watery environment. If our blood, muscles, and organs

---

[9] "the study of the mechanics of body movements" —Google definition

do not receive optimal amounts of water, they will not function at peak performance. The most assimilatable is pure spring, or un-polluted well water, without fluoride or chlorine added! Then water from fresh organic fruits and vegetables.

The amount of water is important: At least 1 ounce per 2 pounds (approx. 1 Kg.) of weight.

SALT AND SUGAR

Salt and sugar are added to most processed foods. Four ounces of sugar a day over a long period is enough to put you at high risk for cardiovascular disease. And most Americans eat much more than that. The average American eats 20 times the salt needed for good health and most, if not all of that, is *unnatural* salt—it has no minerals. Refined/unnatural salt not only does not provide us with the many minerals we need, it actually leaches minerals from the body.

Additives can impede the flow of messages to the nerves, fowl the circulatory system, cause cancer, and adversely affect the heart—plenty of reasons for athletes or anybody for that matter to eat pure, unadulterated, organic food.

PROCESSED FOODS

Today two thirds of the average American diet consists of highly processed foods. Why should we choose fresh as opposed to frozen or canned foods? When we look at just the vitamin aspect of nutrition we can easily see that frozen foods destroy over half the B-vitamins in the processing. Canned peas and beans destroyed more than 75 percent of B5 and B6. Canned green vegetables destroy 50 percent of B5 and B6. If the cans are stored for a long time another 25 percent of the vitamin content is lost. Fresh, organic food is best.

> "Leave the food that man made
>
> Eat the food that God made."
>
> — DR. MARK HYAM

WHOLE FOODS

Whole foods are nature's gift. They contain all the necessary vitamins and minerals needed for their own metabolizing by the body. The common loaf of bread is a useful example. White bread is robbed of most of its nutrients in the processing of the grain into flour to make it white. This bread is so devoid of nutrients necessary for life that even the rodent weevil, which normally thrives on wheat, dies on a diet of white bread. "Enriched" bread may put back some of the nutrients like thiamine, niacin, riboflavin, pantothenic acid, and magnesium, but these are not enough to fully digest the food—Only whole-grain breads contain more nutrients for a healthier body.

LESS MEAT

> "My Body Tiz of Me,
>
> Health is My Victory!"

KURT KRUEGER, PHD (PLAY HAPPILY DAILY)

—BETHANY ARGISLE

The groups of people who live over 100 years with great vitality, like the Hunzakuts, Maya Indians, and East Indian Tatos, have basically the same diet of pure, fresh, and whole foods. Their diet is moderate in protein, while high in complex carbohydrates. The vegetables are fresh daily or bi-daily. Their diet is low in protein while high in complex carbohydrates. They have little, if any, fresh meat in their diet. Russians did not allow their competitors to eat red meat, as red meat is more difficult to digest. Therefore, energy is conserved and able to be channeled into use by the body.

Joe Gonzales, world champion freestyle wrestler, has said, "It is a proven fact that vegetarians have more endurance. The strongest animals in the world are vegetarians." When I heard this kind of statement and read many books on nutrition many years ago, I thought I'd better become a vegetarian. I had a problem, though—I only liked about five vegetables and loved meat. It was my staple having come from German and Swedish lineage. Being an intelligent man, I took it slowly to overcome years of societal conditioning. Luckily, I found a few tasty cookbooks like, *The New Laurel's Kitchen* and *Recipes for a Small Planet*. They helped me to enjoy more vegetables while lessening the amount of meat in my diet. Soon enough the cravings for meat ceased. There are so many books now on this topic. You may want to also try *Whole Life Nutrition Cookbook*.

Yale University medical school did a study on endurance comparing Olympians who were on a high (100 gram or more) meat-protein diet, and non-athletes who had been on a low (less than 50 grams) vegetarian-protein diet. They were surprised to find the non-athletes had better endurance. So they put the Olympians on a 50-gram vegetarian protein diet. The end result showed as much as a 50 percent improvement. Prolav Estavo, the famous clinical nutritionist, had people on a high-meat protein diet exercise to exhaustion, and it took only 30 to 60 minutes. Then, after being on a low-protein, high complex carbohydrate vegetarian diet, they lasted up to four hours. Some of the reasons for this follow:

- Most meat, including poultry and fish, are fed or injected with growth hormones and additives like antibiotics. Steroids are the primary culprit, which is a banned substance for competitors and some are proven to be carcinogenic. One Midwestern farmer was caught feeding his cattle cement to sell at a weightier, and therefore, better price.

- Meat and excess dairy products build up a lot of uric acid and purine which deposits in the joints, causing problems of arthritis and trouble with the kidneys and liver, as well as making us more acidic.

- Once an animal is killed the meat begins to decay. Preservatives are added to slow the decay, some of which have been found to be determents to health and even carcinogenic years later. Some colorings added to hide the look of decaying meat have also been proven to be carcinogenic.

- The U.S. Army found that a high-meat protein diet takes away B3, B6, calcium and magnesium. This creates a lot of imbalances in the body.

- Cholesterol in the blood will be reduced when less meat is eaten and more complex carbohydrates, especially legumes and brown rice, peas, and beans. If you choose to eat meat, make sure it is fresh, free-range and unadulterated, and with cattle – grass fed, and eat less of it. No more than the size of your clinched fist – like Europeans eat!

In effect, eating a diet with meat depletes energy of the body, clogs the nervous system, and is less healthy these days. A proper vegetarian diet will keep more people healthier. A simple vegetarian diet will contain:

- Whole, non-GMO grains—rice, wheat, quinoa, couscous, and so on;

- Fresh organic fruits;

- Organic nuts and seeds;

- Organic vegetables;

- Some honey and other natural lightly refined sweeteners;

- Some dairy, preferably soured such as cheeses, kefir, and yogurt.

This diet contains more elements that form the mind and body, whereas an omnivore eats food which produces more excrement and flesh.

THE RIGHT AMOUNT

What is ingested is not the only element for proper nutrition. Also important is how much we put into the body. It is best to fill the stomach *half-full* with food and one quarter with liquid (preferably pure water). Leave the rest empty for easy digestion. This formula has been handed down for thousands of years as a way to stay healthy. It is also supported by nutritional studies (Weindruch, 1979).

Optimum nutrition should also reduce your appetite. Over-eating is one of the main causes of disease and premature aging. Excess food, beyond the needs of the body, act as a poison in the system. The digestive system is overworked as is the excretory system. Too much energy and blood is used for excess food processing by the body. It could be used for training and building muscles or fighting disease. Stop when you begin to feel content. A decent rule of thumb is a fist-sized serving of protein, vegetables, and so on.

Eating too much also affects your state of mind. It can turn a quick thinker into a slower one, a clear thinker into a muddled thinker. A former academic All-American football player and noted nutritionist, Gabriel Cousens, M.D. recalls, "Whenever I was tempted to overeat because of a favorite food, my mind was not alert so my body could not go through the plays so well. I seemed to play without any spirit." He quickly learned not to overeat. After graduating with honors, he became a nutritional psychiatrist.

At the other extreme, eating too little, without sufficient vitamins and minerals, will adversely affect performance also.

Willie Mays, the Hall of Fame baseball great said, "Dieting makes one nervous, distracting from a player concentrating on his game." When you do choose to cut down on the amount of food eaten, make sure you do it gradually and with a professional's guidance. Reduce the calorie intake by no more than one third and use the proper supplements. See a nutritionist when possible, and eat right to be fit for life.

SUPPLEMENTATION

Supplements are needed to make sure your body has all the necessary vitamins and minerals it needs to be healthy. In hospitals where processed foods are served to patients, they have found more than 75 percent of the patients become malnourished after admittance and not as a result of their illness. Fresh oranges bought at a supermarket were found to contain no vitamin C at all, probably because of transportation, heat, and storage time. Oranges bought from the grower on the day of picking contained an average of 180 mg of vitamin C each. Therefore, the only sure way to have the necessary vitamins and minerals is through daily use of necessary supplements or picking your food daily! But don't overdose on too many supplements. Periodically, check with a nutritionist or chiropractor, or use muscle testing as described in the book, *Your Body Doesn't Lie* by John Diamond for your needs in this area.

Eighty-four percent of Olympic athletes use supplements. In studies done in the Olympic lifts of the clean and jerk and the press, those who took individually-designed supplements improved their performance by four to eight percent respectively. That's enough to raise a top lifter from anonymity to a gold medal. In another study, marathoners improved their times on the average of over 11 minutes, had 35 percent fewer minor injuries, and 81 percent fewer infections than did the placebo control group. This was a six-month study.

Phytochemical supplements work to heal within the cells and are best for everyone—better than vitamin C (but not replacing it). **Some special phytochemicals have been proven to help balance the endocrine system to produce the right amount of needed hormones, recuperate after training, and heal wounds, while others help stimulate the immune system to prevent HIV and cancers or even reverse them.**

NUTRITION AND THE MIND

Nutrition affects reaction times, strength, and endurance. The mind is also dramatically influenced by foods. **Learning, moods, and insomnia are just a few mental areas which are improved through the proper ingestion of nutrients.** The mood affects of food are very real. In a study described by Kagen (1985), neuro-endocrinologist and physician R. Wurtman showed that complex carbohydrates can have the same effect on people as antidepressant drugs. They improve mood, diminish sensitivity to negative stimuli, and ease the way to sleep. At the University of Sussex, psychologist Angus Craig tested pilots and schoolchildren after different kinds of meals. Heavy meals caused a significant drop in reaction time in visual perception in the pilots and made it harder for the children to learn new material (Josephson, 1985). And as food affects your body, it also affects your mind and spirit. A simple example is an athlete who overeats just before a competition. The mind is scattered, preventing concentration, and energy is directed toward digesting the food in the stomach. One cannot produce a spirited performance.

Nutrition and the Spirit

The calming influence specific nutrients have on the mind allow the energy/spirit to express itself more freely. Occidental/Western nutrition investigations are devoid of research on food's influence on the spirit, and vice versa. But indigenous peoples, Indians and Orientals, have applied old wisdom and knowledge in the use of foods for uplifting and freeing the spirit, which in turn produces health and well-being to the practitioner. One must choose a diet according to individual needs, one which supports the body's activities, peace of mind, and stimulates the energy/spirit. A technology developed by Rudolf Steiner (better known for creating Waldorf Education), demonstrates bio-dynamically grown foods have the highest and longest lasting energetic patterns. Likewise, the subtle energy of the spirit can alter the food we ingest. Marcel Vogul, director of the Psychic Research Institute, has actually shown that water with the thought form of love transmitted into it, has a different taste and subtle vibration. This may illustrate the value in the blessing of food or prayer before eating which is prevalent in most cultures. Prayer or silence prior to a meal allows a number of beneficial results to occur:

- The mind begins to focus and calm down.

- The body in turn calms down and begins to ready to experience the fragrant food.

- The spiritual vibrations and the prayers intention are then brought into the food and thus into your body.

- You are less distracted from your previous experience(s) of the day.

There needs to be more research in the area of nutrition at the spiritual level. The studies should probe areas of the influence the spirit has on nutrient qualities, and investigate how the spirit is affected by foods and qualities thereof (for example, frozen, canned, fresh, biodynamic/organic, and so on).

MORE NUTRITIONAL ADVICE

"Let food be thy medicine, and medicine be thy food."

—HIPPOCRATES, *The Father of Medicine*

A few more points for those aspiring to sustained peak performance:

- Pure air, unpolluted by chemicals from business and industry, household chemicals, and so on, is most vital. Yet we allow such toxins to infiltrate our bodies through our skin, lungs, and elsewhere. Simply driving on a freeway of heavily traveled road has so many toxins floating in the air. Use a quality air purifier for your home, office, business, car.

- Water is so important. It supplies the body with necessary blood volume and therefore, oxygen and nutrients to all systems of the body. Dehydration can easily be prevented by drinking a third of a cup of water per half hour of exercise, and at least an ounce (28 g) of water for every kilogram (2.2 pounds) that you weigh.

- Eat at least two to three hours prior to training, competition or an important meeting or event. Eat a light and easily digested and balanced meal. Your blood will be used for the muscles and brain activity rather than for digestion. More energy will be available for your important activity.

- If you are going to binge on food or drink, do it the day after the important activity, and no more than once a week. The body can reduce the amount of toxins ingested during the binge over several days time. But binging is never a practice that benefits your health nor wellbeing.

- Smoking and alcohol are major causes of many degenerative diseases such as cancer, cardiovascular disease, liver, and respiratory diseases. Even if someone regularly smokes near you indoors, your disease risk is that of a 10-cigarettes-a-day smoker. Regular drinkers, of about two drinks per day, have multiple vitamin and mineral deficiencies, including, B3, B6, C, magnesium, zinc, and essential fatty acids. If you do smoke or drink decreasing your consumption should be done for your health and performance. This is made easier when you have proper nutrition, including the necessary vitamin and mineral supplements to overcome any deficiencies.

There is more to the science of nutrition which can affect the mind and spirit of an evolving person. But first let us begin with acting on the ideas proposed in this chapter. Give yourself three months to make positive dietary changes. Use the previous references to enhance your knowledge and give you psychological support during the changeover. You may wish to use an encouraging buddy with this and other positive changes.

FOOD AS SACRED

And finally, the following is taken from the teachings of Swami Muktananda Paramahansa and with the permission of the copyright holder Gurudev Siddha Peeth Ganeshpuri, India 1980. Prepared with love for all by Kurt A. (Narayan) Krueger

Food is the essence of life. It is through food that a person is born. He lives by food, too. And, ultimately he merges into the Earth, which produces food. The most important thing in life is food. It should be treated as sacred.

When a cook treats food as sacred, there is a lot that naturally follows. When you treat food as sacred, you recognize the life

force within it. This energy is conscious. It is what makes food nourishing.

Food is full of bliss. Food is full of life. But, only if you handle it in the right way can you be happy. You should neither eat too much or too little. You should be clean and pure when you cook and you should eat in a clean and pure place. Eat only as much as you can digest. Fill the stomach half with food, a quarter with liquid (preferably pure water) and one quarter left for easy digestion. One who is not disciplined in eating can neither practice yoga, nor be healthy, nor have good thoughts.

While we prepare and eat food, we should repeat our mantra, OM NA-MAH SHI-VA-YA. This mental vibration begins to permeate the body's cells bringing the cellular vibration into harmony, making it function better. The food that goes into us becomes supremely pure. Prepare and eat food in a state of meditation.

In silence, O dear one,

eat without haste.

With peace, delight, and

one-pointedness,

thoroughly chew your food.

Don't eat merely

for the pleasure of taste.

SUMMARY

Eating right correctly and having the proper vitamin and mineral supplementation can keep you healthier and more alert while concurrently improving performance. When you start using proper nutrition, allow at least three months to observe the results, although they will show up sooner in most cases. Twelve months is necessary for the cells of your body to regenerate from properly nourished cells. You will be surprised at the results.

"We are what we repeatedly do.

Excellence then, is not an act, but a habit."

—Aristotle

BOOK THREE ~ Spirit

"The momentous thing in human life is the art of winning the soul to good or evil."

—FRANCIS BACON

[11] MEDITATE EVEN MORE

"The greatest discovery of any generation is that human beings can alter their lives by altering the attitudes of their minds."

—ALBERT SCHWEITZER, NOBEL PEACE LAUREATE

FIVE ELEMENTS

SOME GREAT ATHLETES AND CEOs spontaneously drop into the state of meditation regularly before or during big competitions/situations. This happens because five major elements occur:

1. Relaxation and letting go

2. Concentration

3. Breathing exercises

4. Emptying the mind of thought (meditation)

5. Rhythmic activity

Let's go deeper with the subject of meditation, as it is so beneficial, and integral in *Winning Ways*. As Michael Murphy wrote in *In The Zone: Transcendent Experience in Sports*: "it (the body) is a focusing point, a place to start from, but from this sturdy base we are capable of reaching beyond, of fleshing out the spirit in the areas where the body cannot reach, initiating movements the eye cannot see, revealing strengths that transcend mere muscles, and exerting energies that can no longer be considered physical in the ordinary sense." Years of training in meditation may be required to reach a deep mental state where the powers of the inner "Self" are fully tapped. After studying and practicing many forms of meditation, the one form which has always been effective with people includes a concentration on the breath, awareness of the space between the breath, with a simple cue word.

Traditionally, meditation was only taught by masters to dedicated students or disciples. Of course, these are modern times and "nothing is sacred." The esoteric teachings have seeped out into widespread distribution. Yet the highest experiences elude so many because of the lack of dedicated practice and the guidance by a master. But when we regularly use meditation, we go beyond the mere physical into the supernatural realms of performance as we know them today.

THE FUTURE: A POWER FOR PEACE

Even when we do solve the problems of wars and hunger, the environment and relationships, without peace of mind, we have achieved nothing. As the former Secretary General of the United Nations, U-Thant said, "There is no peace in the world because there is no peace in the minds of men."

There seem to be two ways of solving the age-old problem for accomplishing peace. The first is within oneself and subsequently society, and the next is on an interpersonal and hence, global level. Over the last 30 years researchers have found that when one percent of a population in a town meditated, homicides, car accidents, and suicides all decreased. The crime rate went down. Meditation can, therefore bring peace to oneself and to our cities. In fact, over the years, groups of highly experienced meditators traveled to the troubled spots in the world—Lebanon, South Africa, Nicaragua, and so on. They sat quietly grouped in their hotel and meditated. They did no protest or propaganda for peace. Together, they simply practiced a powerful meditation technique. Within three days, violence dramatically subsided.

When the critical number of meditators left, the violence returned within three days. These experienced meditators did a similar study with violence rates while meeting in Rhode Island during a summer. The auto fatalities and violent crime decreased nearly 50 percent. Within two weeks of leaving their summer conference, the crime and fatality rates returned to normal. According to Gabriel Cousens, M.D., "We urge all like minded people to open their hearts, overcome the sense of difference for a time, and participate in this meditation for planetary peace. Through meditation there is the creation of inner peace which makes it much easier for peace to manifest in our personal lives."

[12] SWITCH HABITS

"Why not create habits that will mint gold?"

—HAFIZ, Persian mystic poet

WITH A NEWFOUND ABILITY to create visions in our lives, to focus, to tap into our potential, and to create the physical health and prowess we desire, wouldn't it be great to commit these positive actions to habit? Some say we are our habits, that our lives and destinies are the accumulation of all we do, good or bad. Creating *good* habits is of obvious benefit, of course, but how do we go about this? How do we create good habits?

Let's look at three *Winning Ways* to go about creating our own pre-determined positive habits:

- First, experts might disagree on the number of days it takes, but the consensus is that if we simply do something every day for long enough (21 days, 60 days, whatever that might be for you), it becomes a *habit,* done without thinking or effort. Simple enough—*just do it!* Do it regularly, and do it enough. Set up regular times to do a fitness regimen, to play, to meditate, and to go to bed. Put positive, constructive, winning ways in place.

- Second, we'll discuss what Greek philosopher and legendary mathematician Pythagoras prescribes.

- Third, I'll share one of my own developments for not only creating good habits but reversing bad ones with a description of "Switching®."

PYTHAGORAS

Most people have heard of the Greek mathematician and philosopher Pythagoras. He would have his students review and preview their day. Now, about 2,500 years later, research in psychology shows that this works very well for improving a person's life. Before sleeping, Pythagoras' students would sit for a short time to review their day's activities. Each student wrote down where improvements and advances were made, with all the positive activities and feeling involved. Being grateful for these many things allows us to focus on the good. This helps to bring about more happiness and health according to current research, and according to the Gratefulness and the Happiness Movements.

Next, Pythagoras' students were instructed to write down where they erred, so the errors may be corrected. With the error page Pythagoras' students would say: "Thank you for letting me see where I get to improve," and tear up the page into fine pieces, placing them in a bin. They would then plan their next day before going off to sleep. It would include important activities for the body, mind, and spirit. It would be in order of priority or time constraints. During the night's sleep, the mind processes the possibilities for the next day and makes a person ready for achieving their mission for the day. This simple activity by these ancient Greeks enabled them to be conscious of their actions and ultimately their thoughts. When this happened they gained more control over their lives. They began to have fewer worries and take more positive actions.

Modern achievement-oriented people and books dealing with the subject would agree that this method is very effective for our modern day, but you might add a few additional *Winning Ways*: Use Pythagoras' practice nightly. Observe how to improve a day's activity for the next day, so you don't have to step into the same holes of conditioned responses. And again, before getting out of bed in the morning imagine your perfectly planned day happening in your mind's eye— Visualize its fulfillment and the feelings this would produce. Then get out of bed with more enthusiasm. See how your work, learning, and social interactions are positively affected. And to make this system of self improvement even more powerful, there are a few more powerful *Winning Ways*— "Afformations®" and "Switching®."

AFFORMATIONS

There are plenty of books on "affirmations," which is the common term for repeating positive phrases in your mind so you and your situations become that which you think. A proverb says, "As a man thinketh in his heart, so is he." When I taught history many years ago, misbehaving students were assigned to write at least 75 times (research showed that was a minimum), in paragraph form, "I am good and I am getting better!" or "I am always on time." With fully-stated affirmations, the whole sentence and therefore the whole thought stays in our minds and our behavior is improved.

But there is an advanced practice, beyond affirmations, described in a book called *Afformations*® by Noah St. John. After hearing about and practicing afformations, I offered students the opportunity to use this instead of affirmations. Afformations® make an affirmation into a question. Thus, "I am happy," becomes, "Why am I so happy?" Or, "I am confident" becomes "Why am I so confident?" Thus, as Socrates has said, the answers will come, and as stated in the Bible, in Matthew 7:7, "Ask and it will be given to you; seek and you will find; knock and the door will be opened to you." Or, for the somewhat scientific-minded, "The vacuum created by the question draws forth the answer."

SWITCHING®

And when it comes to forming good habits, if I were to choose one practice from so many, it would be Switching®. If you would like to change yourself for the better and transform old, bad habits into good ones, you can make use of Switching®, and the more you use it the faster it works! **The best way to go through life is to focus on what you *want* rather than follow the definition of insanity** (to do the same thing over and over again and expect different results).

Let's reverse negative tendencies, and let's include the body in with the mental and spiritual practice. Research shows that negativity suppresses the immune system, and research proves that simply praising and/or encouraging a person raises blood sugar levels, perks you up, the immune system is enhanced, and you feel better. Yet people continue the same old habits because they haven't focused on something that can really change their habits for the better. Many of us don't know how to change that old pattern, or we would have long ago.

We speak internally to ourselves, sometimes in a positive way and yet all too often in a way that is degrading to ourselves and/or others. When we start to notice this self-talk becoming negative, or when we find ourselves practicing any kind of undesirable habit, we can simply say to ourselves, "switch!" and rephrase the negative into a positive afformation. Our belief system is built on what we *regularly* say to ourselves, so make all self-talk positive and with a question. For example, if I think to myself, "I always lose my races at the end," and I catch myself say this, I immediately say, "Switch! Why do I finish my race with a great burst of speed?" Switching® is a simple, powerful, and effective way to change old habit patterns. It uses all the essential elements for learning and un-learning:

- physical,

- mental,

- spiritual,

- audio,

- visual,

- and kinetic.

And in a constant search for ever more *Winning Ways*, I felt that better results could be achieved by bringing more senses into Switching®. I began to teach people to use their hands while saying "switch," elbows at the side, forefingers pointed skyward, near the shoulders, allowing them to cross in front of the body, fingers pointing in opposite directions to eliminate the old pattern. It worked better. A 14 year-old boy, who sucked his thumb a lot each day, used this practice and stopped within two weeks. Others experienced similar reversals of bad habits. I felt that I was onto something.

Why not expand on the psycho-somatic efforts with a little energetic reversal? Our habits create a movement of energy that I feel is somewhat associated with the movement of the Earth. It's like wind flowing in a vortex. To utilize the power of the wind, we can be like sailors tacking against the wind and soon enough the pattern of the wind changes with the efforts of Switching® and we can then flow with the new pattern of positive thoughts.

I then asked people to place the left hand fingers skyward, palm facing your face, with the right palm against it, and rotate these connected hands in a counterclockwise direction, and switch the negative idea. Change it into its opposite by mentally or verbally repeating its positive replacement Afformation, like, "Why am I so healthy?" or "Why am I so happy?" and so on. This again expedited the desired results.

And with these encouraging experiences, I then applied a practice of gratitude. I asked people to include, "Thank you." This announced to the mind or "inner Self" that you were thankful for remembering to transform the negative thought into positive experience, to be more in control of your life, thus, choosing to create the life you know is best for you and for others. And, being a spiritual person, I say, "Thank you God."

Once you have Switched any lower- or negative-energy thinking, you then want to "zip" the positive force of your inner Afformation® into your new awareness. Simply place your right little finger at the base of your torso between your legs, lift your hand horizontally up the center of your body, up above your head and bring it back down to your right side, in the shape of a large "D" as you say, "Thank you, I love you." You have just sealed in your afformation with your chosen thought. It's like you've zipped up the new awareness of the new *you* that you are creating—it is now part of you, you are thankful, and you love the new *you*! And who are you loving? You, God, and the ability to begin to create a life of your choice. Pretty simple, eh? All it takes is consistent practice, and soon enough, it will seldom, if ever, have to be used for that issue.

NEXT STEPS

Find a buddy and/or work with a team. During some of the time you spend together support each other's development toward your new habits and goals for life. If you have a habit that has to change according to you, then for sure, get a buddy to work with, especially one that you see quite regularly. It could be a family member.

Let's say you wished to stop smoking or drinking. Your friend or relative, when they see you starting for a cigarette, could signal you to switch by crossing their hands in the Switching® motion. You then see this, put the cigarette back, and do the full Switching® routine. Likewise, you could help your friend or relative get into the Switching® routine themselves. We literally start to consciously control our own life when we practice Switching® and the more we use Switching® the more power we may exert in our life, the more loving we may be with others, the more unbounded we are! Each time that you use Switching® you experience more strength to create the life that you choose. You begin to act more like the person you always wanted to be!

[13] PRACTICE YOGA

"To get something you've never gotten, you have to do
something you've never done."

—Attributed to CAM NEWTON AND OTHERS

ONE FORM OF EXERCISE satisfying all three human
needs of physical, mental, and spiritual fitness is yoga. It was
developed over 3,000 years ago as a practice of keeping the
body fit while calming and strengthening the mind, and
accessing the inner spirit. Many descriptions of supernatural
feats by both the yogis and martial arts masters have
permeated the literature throughout history.

Beyond the Relaxation Response describes studies done by
Herbert Benson in India indicating dramatic increases in
external body temperature while the internal was kept normal;

according to the Menninger Foundation's research with Swami Rama and others.

HATHA[10] YOGA

My first class in Yoga was with Yogi Bhajan in 1970. He used Hatha Yoga as a means to awaken the Kundalini (spirit power). He had us do a posture called the "boat" for five minutes straight. I couldn't do it, even though I was fit enough to have had three swimming school records at the University of Colorado. I quit doing Yoga at the time because I liked to be successful, but I did pick it up again and have been practicing Hatha Yoga now since 1973. Hatha Yoga is a form of static stretching[11] for toning and strengthening the whole body while focusing the mind. This has kept me supple and strong, while toning all of my bodily systems.

In researching its applications for living, I found an amazing example from sports. A high school football team had used yoga for seven years as warm-ups and cool-downs and special ones when they came off the field during a game, and not a single player missed a game because of a muscle injury. In six years of consistent winning records, they lost a

---

[10] "Hatha simply refers to the practice of physical yoga postures, meaning your Ashtanga, Vinyasa, Iyengar and Power Yoga classes are all Hatha Yoga. The word "hatha" can be translated two ways: as "willful" or "forceful," or the yoga of activity, and as "sun" (ha) and "moon" (tha), the yoga of balance." —www.yogajournal.com/category/yoga-101/types-of-yoga/hatha/

[11] Static stretching is used to stretch muscles while the body is at rest. It is composed of various techniques that gradually lengthen a muscle to an elongated position (to the point of discomfort) and hold that position for 30 seconds. —Wikipedia

total of only four games. Mr. Jerry Colletto, the coach, suggests that these warm-ups and cool-downs keep you healthy and focus the mind, thus preparing it for competition. The Pittsburgh Steelers football team used a stretch coach when they were winning Super Bowls.

I've met people from all walks of life coming to the courses I taught for various Southern California colleges. Each one of them found that Hatha Yoga was extremely easy and pleasant to practice. It is great for reducing stress in the body and mind, and an invigorating exercise series for starting a day or for mellowing out after work—a kind of preventative medicine, and even more.

In my years of study and training athletes and people in business and government, I have found the most effective method for overcoming negative stress in the body to be Hatha Yoga. It is a physical activity geared to an individual's capacity for stretching and being still. It is not about tying yourself into a pretzel. Anyone can learn it and once learned, you can appreciate it anywhere when you feel yourself getting uptight or stressed-out.

The benefits of Hatha Yoga cover a vast range:

- It tones all the systems of the body—especially the endocrine, cardiovascular, and respiratory;

- Stretches the muscles in preparation for training and preventing injuries;

- Releases the physiological effects of stress;

- Stimulates the body to achieve its proper weight;

- Super concentrates the mind while relaxing the body.

All these benefits are useful for the average person as well as the elite competitor or business person. If you cannot find an expert yoga teacher, you may easily acquire these lucid texts on Amazon:

- *Hatha Yoga for Meditators*, by Swami Dayananda (SYDA Foundation, New York, 1981),

- *Integral Yoga Hatha*, (July 15, 2002) by Sri Swami Satchidananda.

- *Light on Yoga*, (1995) B.K.S. Lyengar and Yehudi Menuhin

These are books written with a holistic approach—ones that train the body, mind, and spirit for ultimate performance.

ASANA[12] (YOGA POSTURES) INTRO

The following exercises stretch, tone, and strengthen the body, while focusing the mind and opening a person to spiritual energy. The following Hatha Yoga routine of poses is developed to work out the whole body. Practice them at your own ability, move into each position with only pressure—no pain.

Your state of mind is of paramount importance in performing any asana. Release the ego that says, "I am doing the postures." Merely watch the body move into the

---

[12] An "asana" is simply "a posture adopted in performing hatha yoga." —Google definition

144

appropriate position. Stay in a place inside yourself where nothing is happening at all. It is best to have a qualified instructor of traditional Hatha Yoga to learn the following practices. Find a person who has had a master teacher, not someone who has simply learned from books.

Wait two to three hours after a meal to workout with these exercises, as this allows the blood to oxygenate so you vitalize the whole body, not just the stomach. Practice the HUM-SO concentration/meditation technique with each position. The success of asanas is dependent upon your being relaxed, calm, and centered. If you had just one exercise to use for fitness and/or warm-ups or cool-downs, it should be the Sun Salutation of Hatha Yoga. (Full instructions for this excellent form is detailed in BOOK TWO, chapter "[8] Warm-Up & Cool-Down.") It is a simple and vastly effective practice; it can be done at an aerobic or anaerobic rate; it tones and stretches the muscles, thus preventing injury; it stimulates the internal organs while it refines the functioning of the glands, thus promoting health; it focuses the mind and opens oneself to the inherent spirit—all this while stimulating the effective flow of energy within the body.

Specific postures (asanas) of Hatha Yoga may be practiced for various sports or a particular fitness regime. Yoga postures each have a curative and/or preventative ability for stimulating health and well-being down to the organ level. If you have a particular organ health issue, you may consult such a Yogini/Yogi.

Yoga prepares us for physical exertion and loosens every part of the body. Our breathing capacity is developed, while the spine becomes flexible and strong. The various movements stimulate the entire body, including all the systems, especially the muscular, endocrine, circulatory, respiratory, and digestive. The gentle stretching greatly assists in loosening the joints and muscles of the legs and back. The synchronization of the movements and the balanced rhythm of the breath develops coordination and breath control. It is also a great eye exercise. The SS Stretch can be used as a workout when done rapidly for 20 minutes or as preparation and/or culmination of a training or competition session, when done slowly. As a warm-up, begin the SS Stretch slowly, increasing the speed while doing 7 to 12 repetitions. As a cool-down, begin as fast as the breath moves, slowing down as you do at least seven repetitions.

PREPARATION FOR ASANAS

During each of the following, to receive the MAXIMUM benefit from each posture (asana), be mindful/aware of:

1. Use the mantra with each breath.

2. As you bend forward breathing out with the mantra, pay attention to releasing the tension in that particular muscle(s) being stretched.

3. While staying in the stretch, allow the in-breath to open/expand the muscles being stretched. Sense/feel the vibration that this can create.

4. Tighten the opposing muscle. That sends a message to the brain that it is a desired 'extreme' stretch, and the body will stretch even further.

5. As you bend backward breathing in with the mantra, pay attention to releasing the tension in that particular muscle(s) being stretched.

6. Know that the repetition of the mantra will send its harmonious vibrations throughout your whole body through the blood. Thus bringing each cell into a balanced/harmonious vibration.

7. Be sure your body is in proper alignment because if not, your asana can actually be somewhat detrimental to you, similar to what misaligned tires do to the car.

CORPSE (SAVASANA)

Allows the body to completely prepare for and to simulate the benefits from each of the fitness postures while the energy flows freely throughout the body in a relaxed and unimpeded movement. It brings relaxation to the body as there is no stress put upon the spine, muscle structure, nor internal organs. The corpse pose allows the full absorption of the benefits of the previous session. Always follow a fitness session with 5 to 15 minutes of this posture.

1. Lie on the floor, palms upward comfortably near the hips.
2. Lift your pelvis slightly off the floor then relax it to the floor.
3. Relax both outstretched legs about shoulder width apart.
4. Consciously release any tension in the body. Focus on the breath with HUM-SO breathing.

Video: https://www.youtube.com/watch?v=v1IkTK16XUQ

TRIANGLE (TRIKONASANA)

For the sides (lateral) stretching and toning, helps to trim the waist. It aids in digestion and elimination by gently massaging the muscles and abdominal organs. Keep the legs stress-free and flexible while strengthening and stretching the buttocks and lower back.

1. Stand comfortably erect with the feet shoulder width or slightly more apart.

2. Turn the left foot in a 30 degrees angle and the right foot out 90 degrees.

3. For correct balance, place the heel of the right foot directly in line with the middle of the left foot.

4. Breathe in mentally repeating HUM while slowly raising the arms shoulder height extended out parallel on either side, palms facing down.

5. Exhale mentally as you repeat SO and slowly twist your body to the right, simultaneously reaching toward your right foot with your left hand.

6. As you do this, keep your right arm relaxed and extended straight upward and turn your head to look toward it.

7. Breathe deeply HUM-SO with each in and out breath and holding this position for a count of 11 or more—up to 2 minutes max.

8. Then breathe deeply in as you mentally repeat HUM while returning to a standing position. First, extend your arms outward and then lower them to your sides.

9. Relax and repeat to the other side.

Video: https://www.youtube.com/watch?v=VLEiXbEJCM4

Shoulder Stand (Salamba Sarvangasana)

Maintains metabolic vitality by bringing oxygenated blood to the brain, thyroid, and parathyroid glands. It provides a gentle massage of the thyroid, and parathyroid glands with each breath because of the constriction of the neck. Stretches the upper back and neck releasing the tensions. Lymphatic toxins stored in the legs are drained. It promotes good blood circulation, calms the nerves by stimulating the parasympathetic nervous system, decreases depression and anxiety symptoms, eases fatigue, and improves immune function.

1. With a four-folded blanket under your shoulders, lie in the corpse pose with the HUM-SO breath calmly flowing through you, consciously relaxing your body/mind.

2. SO-exhale while slowly raising your legs six inches. Take a full breath, then continue raising the legs to a 45-degree angle, arms and palms (on the floor) outstretched along your torso for a full HUM-SO breath, then continue upward until the legs are perpendicular to the floor.

3. Lift your legs, hips, and trunk to a vertical position while simultaneously raising your forearms and positioning your hands on your lower back for support as your elbows are resting triangularly on the ground.

4. With the chin pressed against your chest, allow your entire body from the neck to the toes to be as relaxed and straight as possible. The back of your head, neck, shoulders and upper arms and elbows should rest firmly on the blanket and floor.

5. Breathe normally with HUM-SO and hold this position for the count of 15 to 30 in-breaths—up to 2 minutes max.

6. To come down, SO-exhale and let go of your back and allow it to gracefully return to the floor, vertebrae by vertebrae in a balanced sequence. Continue, and lower your legs to the floor into the corpse position.

7. Rest with the HUM-SO breathing for the length of time you were up in the shoulder stand.

8. Always follow the shoulder stand with the FISH to open, stimulate and flush out the thyroid and parathyroid glands.

Video: https://www.youtube.com/watch?v=1OeRz62g5rw

FISH (MATSYASANA)

Opens the abdomen, chest, and neck area for stimulated flow of oxygen to enhance the internal glands and organs. The thyroid and parathyroid gland is regulated, and the chest greatly expanded, this encourages deep respiration and increased lung capacity, which is highly beneficial for alleviating respiratory ailments. This stimulates the muscles of the eyes—both tightening and relaxing them.

1. From the corpse pose, bring the legs together.

2. Arch your back and head up and backward as you HUM–inhale, placing the top of your head (as close as comfortable to the forehead)on the floor. Looking up and back into the head—this is also an eye exercise.

3. Concurrently, bring your hands to the sides of your hips to brace yourself with the elbows on the ground close to the torso beneath the arched back.

4. With HUM-SO, breathe deeply and expand your chest. Hold for half as long as the shoulder stand.

5. To come down, gently raise the head slightly as you SO–exhale, and allow the back and head to straighten back to the corpse position. Rest in the corpse position for as long as you were in the shoulder stand and fish poses combined.

Video: https://www.youtube.com/watch?v=Xrd8Ghx0W4U

LION POSE (SIMHASANA)

Stimulates the facial muscles, tones the tongue, stretches the eye, throat, jaw, shoulders and lower back muscles, and the major muscles of the body. It also exercises the muscles of the eyes.

1. Assume a kneeling position with the hips on your folded feet. Place your hands on your knees or ground near the knees so that your fingers are extended outwards and you are leaning slightly forward.

2. Extend the tongue outward as far as possible and turn the eyes upward and towards the middle of the forehead.

3. Exhale the breath as much as possible and contract the throat muscles as you make the forceful and LOUD sound of a lion forcefully and loudly.

4. Make the entire body as taut as possible, as if you were a lion about to spring.

5. Stop, release, and then relax. Repeat this asana about three or five times.

Video: https://www.youtube.com/watch?v=yE98pLU4Q7g

HEAD KNEE POSTURE (PASCHIMOTTANASANA)

The Head Knee Posture stretches and tones the backside of the body, especially the hamstrings and lumbar-sacrals. It also stimulates the internal organs—especially the liver, kidneys, and pancreas; trims the waist and relaxes the neck and lower back.

1. From the corpse pose, bring your feet together. As you breathe in with HUM, move your hands along the floor outstretching overhead, thus elongating your body to its full length.

2. Sit up as you breathe out with SO, stretching your head and arms toward the ceiling to open the spine.

3. As you are ready to breathe out again, lean forward with SO, bending your entire upper body forward from the hips as you reach your hands toward your toes and chin toward the knees.

4. Breathe deeply with HUM-SO and hold this position for a count of at least 11 breaths. Before you return to the starting position, stretch a bit further while you tighten your abdominals (abs) – you will be surprised that you will be able to increase the flexibility in this manner. NOTE: The tightening of the opposing muscles "tells" the brain, "it's ok – don't worry – I want to stretch further so release the tension!" Do this on all the static Hatha Yoga practices.

5. Inhaling with HUM, slowly return to the upright sitting position with your arms once again extended upward.

6. Do this twice and return to relax in the corpse position for a minute.

HALF SPINAL TWIST (ARDHA MATSYENDRASANA)

Massages the internal organs, especially the kidneys, and the whole digestive, endocrine and sympathetic nervous systems. It activates the pancreas and tones the nerves of the back. It is allows more nourishment to reach the spinal nerves while bringing spinal flexibility and relief. Helps increase the oxygen supply to the lungs and opens the chest. Exercises the eye muscles.

1. From the corpse position bring the feet together. SO– exhale and rise up into the sitting position with the head and arms reaching high as to the sky.

2. Bending the right knee, place the right foot flat on the floor outside of your extended left knee to bring your left heel alongside the right buttock.

3. Keep the lower leg outstretched until you acquire enough flexibility in this posture, then bend the left knee to bring your left heel against the right buttock.

4. Extend the spine from the lower back. Gently twist the upper body to the right, bring your left arm over the outside of the right knee toward the right foot.

5. Place the right hand behind the back flat on the floor and look as far to the right over the right shoulder. Keep your shoulder as far to the right as possible while "trying" to get your chin twisted around to touch your shoulder. Try to look as far to the right as possible (as if to see your ear).

6. Hold the pose for the count of 15 to 30 in-breaths.

7. Repeat to the opposite side.

Video: https://www.youtube.com/watch?v=0TSarYIMLyA

Cobra (Bhujangasana)

For the front side, toning and stretching the chest and abdomen, aiding in deepening the breath while stimulating the circulation. It is very effective for balancing and strengthening the thyroid and parathyroid glands with their effects on the production of adrenaline and noradrenaline (NA, also called "norepinephrine" or NE). The cobra exercises the deep and superficial muscles of the back, allowing the spine to become stronger and more supple while firming the buttocks. Soothes sciatica, opens the heart and lung areas. It is helpful in relieving backache and abdominal stress caused by tension, overwork, flatulence, and more. It exercises the eye muscles.

1. Lie face-downward with your forehead touching the floor. Breathe fully for the count of 10, relaxing all the muscles of your body.

2. Place your palms firmly on the floor directly below the corresponding shoulders, fingers facing forward, elbows raised and close to your trunk.

3. Inhale deeply with HUM as you slowly use the muscles of the back and buttocks and then raise your head and upper body by arching the back gracefully backward as you gently push up, feeling the stretch of the vertebrae, one by one.

4. As you bend backward, tighten the buttocks (gluteus maximus) to relieve pressure on the lower back. The lower body from the pelvis to the toes remains on the floor.

5. Breathe normally with HUM-SO mantra for the count of 15 to 30 out-breaths and then slowly come down lowering the body as you breathe out with SO, lowering each vertebrae from the base in succession up to the head. Feel this movement of the vertebrae as the breath goes out.

Video: https://www.youtube.com/watch?v=sgC-zvFVHXY

BOAT (NAVASANA)

Good abdominal strengthener and toner, stimulates the digestive system, improves balance, stimulates the kidneys, thyroid and prostate glands and intestines, aids in stress relief, improves confidence.

1. Lie on your back in the corpse pose. Upon exhalation with SO, raise your legs and torso off the ground and spread your straight legs to a 45° angle.

2. The body forms a V with the point of the spine in contact with the ground.

3. Stretch your arms forward between your spread legs at knee height.

4. Hold for about 15 to 30 out-breaths. Don't strain. Return back to the corpse position with the in-breath HUM.

5. Repeat 3 or more times.

Video: https://www.youtube.com/watch?v=vKqdU3rIibU

[14] LOVE

"Love is not automatic. It takes conscious practice and awareness, just like playing the piano or golf. However, you have ample opportunities to practice. Everyone you meet can be your practice session."

—DOC CHILDRE and SARA PADDISON,

PERHAPS THE GREATEST of all *Winning Ways* is *Love*. My greatest teacher, Muktananda, offers his words on Love for your thoughtful benefit. I pray that you get as much from it as I continue to:

~

"You do not have to obtain Love from outside by difficult practices. Its springs lie within. Let your heart overflow with Love. Let your Love be all-encompassing. If you continue to live Love, more of it will be released within. The more you give, the more you will have. He who gives Love is greeted everywhere by Love.

"Give to others what you have inside that is worth giving. Give them the purified parts of yourself, such as courage, knowledge, joy and Love. Love is the only way to cultivate Love.

"There is so much Love in the heart that it is enough not only for one man, but for the whole of humankind. Unfortunately, people do not have access to it because of desire, unnecessary mentation and anxiety. It is only when one becomes completely selfless that the inner spring of ambrosial Love is released.

"Love all with motiveless, desire-less, unsurpassed, unlimited Love. Make Love your life. Become a Love addict. Just Love and Love then Love some more. Freely, godlike, give of yourself.

—Adapted from *Play of Consciousness*, Muktananda, Harper & Row, 1978, edited from pages 237 to 249. Condensed and shared for educational purposes by Kurt Krueger with permission of Swami Muktananda and the copyright holder, Shree Gurudev Ashram, Ganeshpuri, India.

CONCLUSION: IS ANYTHING POSSIBLE?

con·clu·sion (kənˈklooZHən), noun.

1. The end or finish of an event or process: "The conclusion of World War Two." Synonyms: end, ending, finish, close, termination, windup, cessation.

2. A judgment or decision reached by reasoning: "Each research group came to a similar conclusion." Synonyms: deduction, inference, interpretation, reasoning. (Source: Google)

WITH MOST BOOKS, we understand the "Conclusion" to be the final chapter or end of the story, in which case definition number one above would apply. I hope however, this is not the case with you and with your introduction to *Winning Ways*. I'm sure you can see how this new paradigm and how these first *Winning Ways* are only a beginning, and I pray that as you leave this first set of writings on the subject that you will apply definition number *two* above, and start to draw your own conclusion—that so much more is possible through optimum living than you considered previously. To tip you in the right direction as you prepare to put this book down (albeit to refer to again and again) and move on to more discovery, let me prompt you with a question, hopefully thought-provoking and ideally life-changing:

The world is about performance. We must perform at all levels of our life. We are judged by our performance from our first step to our success in school, sports, business and work, socially, and even in our love life. Everyone wishes to be successful, but who is truly trained for total success? Who has the tools for having a fit and healthy body? Who has the tools for a strong mind unaffected by the stresses of the modern world? Who has the tools for accessing the indwelling spirit for enthusiasm and joy in our daily activities? Who has been truly educated and trained for success? Look around at our social systems—not one of them trains a person to fully use the body, mind, and spirit. Our education system avoids speaking about mental training except in the form of simple memorization and regurgitation of facts, hypotheses, and theories. It totally neglects the spirit of the student, especially the non-athlete, because you never hear it spoken, much less see methods for accessing it taught in the classroom. History has proven that we are greater than we think we are. We are capable of great feats of intelligence, strength, endurance, and skill. Humans are called *homo* ("man") *sapiens*, from "sapient" which means "wise, wise man." When we feed our body, mind, and spirit properly, and turn within to the source of wisdom and power, we gain tremendous abilities.

So here's the question:

Is anything possible? Can humans achieve just about anything? What are the limits in this physical world? Is there anything you cannot do? Remember, at one time the world was flat and everyone "knew" it. It took 200 years before people accepted that it wasn't flat *after* such was proven by scientists and world circumnavigators. My exploration in answering this question began as a youth. With the motto, "Attempt and Achieve," I tried all sorts of things from exotic foods to trying my best at a variety of sports. So let's close the first door this book has hopefully opened for you and open some new ones with a few more stories to spark your imagination. Think of what these anecdotes could mean for you.

LIFTING CARS

At 17½ years old, Ken (my twin brother) and I decided to join a club swim team rather than simply train at San Fernando Park Pool. The team we joined, Verdugo Hills Swim Club, had three world record holders. Suddenly, we were guppies swimming with sharks! We had 90-minute workouts led by coach Don Sonia (who later was inducted into the US Swimming, Coaches Hall of Fame). Once after a hard workout in the rain, Ken was driving us home on Interstate 5 at about 65 miles an hour. On a slight curve, we started to fishtail—the rear of the car sliding toward the guardrail four lanes away. I calmly told Ken to slow down. He put his foot on the brakes. This caused the car to spin out of control crossing four lanes of oncoming traffic. As I said some "unkind" words to Ken, we hit the guardrail, and ended up facing forward again. The car was totaled. Ken and I were banged up, but basically okay.

When the tow truck driver came to remove our vehicle from the disaster, he asked if we could pick up the car! I said yes, thinking that Ken and I would do it. Ken was standing blank eyed staring ahead, in a state of shock. I picked up the car, the driver put two tires beneath the rear and towed us away. How did a skinny youth, tired after an intense workout, pick up a car? Most people would say adrenaline made me do it. I accepted this explanation until I studied the field of peak performance practices later in life and developed *Winning Ways*, and now know that if I could do it, so can you! After all, we are in the same human race!

BEYOND THE QUARK

In 1983 I was teaching a history unit on Japan at Louis Pasteur Junior High School. At the time I read Kalie Khalsa's masters degree study, *Beyond the Quark: Gravity and the Mind*, which described three men, each standing on weighing scales. The total of the three scales was 495 pounds. Two of the men picked up the third, a man named Starr, and when they did their two scales then totaled 495 pounds. Putting him down, Starr did a martial arts practice called *rooting*—focusing his energy down through his body into the center of the Earth. Kalie, in her thesis explained that she thought Starr would have "gained weight" in doing so, but he didn't. And when the two other (strong) men tried to pick Starr up while Starr was "rooted," they could not! Ms. Khalsa's conclusion follows:

"The results of the rooting experiment challenge a basic assumption of science that everything happens through interaction or mutual exchange. 'Energy cannot be created or destroyed' is a law of physics which is based on this assumption. This is a four-dimensional assumption about a multidimensional universe, which limits our perception and the discovery of our own potential. Einstein said that we can only see what we believe we can see. He recognized that our pre-established beliefs limit or precede discovery, relative to the situation and perspective of the observer."

Being of adventurous spirit, I described this to my history class as an example of the Japanese notion of "ki," or *spirit power*. I asked two big football players to come and pick me up (we didn't have scales), to put me down, and when I nodded my head, to then pick me up again. I had never rooted in my life, yet they couldn't pick me up! They were surprised but I wasn't. Try it yourself! And I replicated this example 32 years later, in July 2015 in a public program, "Peak Performance Practices" for the Witwatersrand University Sports Department in Johannesburg, South Africa. Prior to the big public talk, I asked Mr. Carter, the sports director, what his goal for the talk was. He simply said, "Show them that they have no limits."

Part way through the presentation, I repeated the rooting experiment, without the scales, explaining that Newtonian physics is passé, could not justify this result, and that quantum physics rules! I explained the energy was connected to the center of the Earth and to pick me up would be like picking yourself up by your own bootstraps! We can only see so much of the visual spectrum, hear only a certain bandwidth of sound waves. Our physical experience of life is so limited, yet when we tap into the unseen and unfelt, what are our limitations? God only knows!

When we tap into the spiritual realm—the unseen—we may access unknown powers. Star Wars calls it the Force; Japanese say "ki;" Chinese say "chi;" Christians call it the Holy Spirit; and physicists say "beyond the quark." Whatever we call it, if I can do it, so can you!

ON BEING GREAT

So again, I ask, is anything possible? We *can* become great in our everyday efforts, so why settle for less? Why not become all we can be? We all know that we have tremendous potential—we have each likely tapped into it at one time or another and have felt the ecstasy of it. Remember for a moment the delight of creative insight, the moment of peak performance in sports or in the arts, the wonder and power at the birthing of a child, the engulfing pleasure at the orgasmic moment? These are just a few peak performance moments in a lifetime. Can our whole life be more like these moments? Can we consciously access our potential creativity and energy, enthusiasm and power, intellect and inspiration, ecstasy and intuition? In following *Winning Ways* we can! We will be able to create the physical, emotional, mental, and spiritual conditions needed to sustain peak performance. After much practice of *Winning Ways*, and we need the peak performance, the performance is ours. If a skinny teenager can (like I was, and where this all started), you can too.

"Inhale the present,

exhale the past."

—KIMBERLYSNYDER.COM

#beautyinsideout

COMPILATION VOLUME

BONUS MATERIAL

MORE WINNING WAYS!

"Practice being rather than knowing. Knowing has gotten you where you are, but being who you really are will get you through the challenges."

—KURT A. KRUEGER

THE *WINNING WAYS* PRESENTED thus far are just the beginning! There are so many more to share and it's my hope that you will continue your journey with them, and that we might meet at a live event or with coaching. To excite your interest in continuing, and with the hope of meeting you in the future, here are some additional and advanced *Winning Ways* we plan to delve into more deeply in future publications and events. Enjoy!

HIGH TECHNOLOGY

One of my colleagues, Brother Charles and Cannon, exposed me to the high technology of modern brain research in 1984. High technology includes special technology from virtual reality, audio/video tapes, and more which enable us to dramatically aid our mental training and abilities as well as heal the body more rapidly. Researchers on the cutting edge of science have found that sound phasing and brain synchronization will access the subconscious very quickly. This technology is used to program positive thoughts (As James Allen wrote, "As we think, so we are.") into our brains, so we receive positive results in our actions. Much of the high technology we use is as developed by Bob Monroe and Brother Charles and M.S.H. Associates. Brother Charles and I created a *Winning Ways* synchronicity audiotape in 1988 (now in digital format) to incorporate it successfully into our peak performance trainings. I used it successfully that year with some Olympians—in Seoul!

The most provocative innovations in using the brain and mind come from both the newest technologies and time-honored methods for tuning the brain, rejuvenating and healing the body, for accessing the mind and programming it for peak performance on a sub-conscious level. Let's take two examples of this technology and leave the rest for later discussion, investigation, and application:

TRANSCUTANEOUS ELECTRICAL NERVE

STIMULATOR (TENS)

Transcutaneous Electrical Nerve Stimulator device (TENS), has at least three highly useful benefits for rejuvenation, healing and sports:

- Faster healing,

- Pain reduction,

- Tuning the mind into the alpha/delta brain range for a peak performance state of mind.

The TENS is an extremely sensitive instrument which produces electromagnetic energy (micro-amps of electricity) similar to the electricity that permeates and sustains the body's cells. The cellular membrane is electrically charged. The area of injury or ill-health has cells which have a lower level of conductivity—a greater amount of resistance happens in that area. So healing is very slow, or doesn't happen at all. These machines are like an external nervous system in that they boost the current around the injured area. Imagine the electromagnetic current flowing in your body like water down a river and you get to the site of the injury, which is like a dam. The energy provided by the TENS breaks through the dam and allows the body's own conductivity or electricity to flow freely again. Consequently, as Becker found in his research, the body rejuvenates/heals at a more rapid rate.

Using the variety of intensities of charge the TENS device can produce will offer a different desired effect. Electro-narcosis, or Alpha Sleep produced by the TENS device, induces a sense of deep relaxation, heightened awareness, an overall sense of well being. This is a state in which you are receptive to healing, and most important for competitors, a brain activity associated with peak performance, and for the rest of us who would love a peak experience state. In bio-chemical terms, alpha sleep causes the release of endorphins in the brain. This reduces pain as endorphins are the body's opiates.

Other frequencies release other brain chemicals—for example, 8 hertz produces serotonin. The center of the brain that releases endorphins is the same center that gives us a sense of pleasure and controls our learning and memory functions. Research by Kirsh described in *The Journal of Electromedicine* has found that electro stimulation of the brain stem may result in heightened attention, alertness and drive. Stimulate this center and we learn and retain new skills faster and more pleasurably. More research needs to be done here for optimum living.

WHOLE BRAIN SYNCHRONY

Second, the easiest technology to use for performance and sports comes from the research initiated at the Monroe Institute of Applied Science and further evolved by M.S.H. Associates. It involves the use of sound patterning for brain synchronization and can be applied using audio or video tapes with stereophonic headsets. The use of headsets also produces an electromagnetic energy balancing of the brain similar to alpha sleep. The patterning sound on the tape enables the brainwaves to be brought into predetermined frequencies, from alpha, theta, down to delta. When the brain waves are in these frequencies, the subconscious is "opened" and affirmations for performance enhancement may be audibly or subliminally communicated. The theory behind this is that the brain can then be scripted with positive thoughts overpowering, after a time, the old negatively conditioned ideas of self doubt, fears, and so on. The constancy in whole brain synchrony brought about by using this technology accesses more of the brain, therefore, we reach more of our potential.

CLASSICAL YOGA

Yoga is union. Yoga is skill in action. Yoga is harmony. Equilibrium is yoga. The science of yoga was first codified about 200 BC by the sage, Patanjali. Before that, the teachings were passed on orally. The primary requisite for the attainment of yoga is the control of the mind or by transcending the mind. Many forms of yogic practices are available for the varied personality types.

As mentioned, I have been practicing yoga for decades, and have studied under masters. The world of yoga has been briefly touched upon in this introductory series, with so much more to learn and teach, for so many wonderful reasons. Watch for more books on the subject and visit my website for opportunities to attend live workshops in your area. In future written works and events we will study and practice *Classical Yoga* as taught by the masters, which includes the types listed below (we touched upon Hatha Yoga and Dhyana Yoga [meditation] in this volume).

- MANTRA YOGA: The repeating of a forceful word(s), for active thinkers;

- RAJA YOGA: The control of the mind's activity, for passive thinkers;

- HATHA YOGA: The pure body Yoga, for the physically active/passive, a branch of Raja also called Asthanga Yoga;

- KARMA YOGA: The will power Yoga of action and service, for the physically active;

- JNANA YOGA: The head power Yoga of Knowledge, for the intellectual type;

- BHAKTI YOGA: The heart Yoga of Love and Devotion, for those emotional types;

- SIDDHA YOGA: The Yoga of Perfected Masters. It encompasses all forms of Yoga as the Guru guides the student with whichever form is useful at the time. A Siddha has the ability to awaken the Kundalini, Spiritual Force, which then guides the practitioner when the Guru isn't physically present.

MUSCLE TESTING

In the mid-1970s I learned to do "muscle testing" as alternative medicine doctors and chiropractors called it, or as the initial medical writer on the subject, Dr. John Diamond, wrote in *Behavioral Kinesiology*. He also wrote a book for the layperson called, *Your Body Doesn't Lie*. I typically used the information in this book to find the best brand, type, and dosage of supplementation for someone, given their ailments, or physical needs. When I started teaching my course in Peak Performance Practices in the early 1980s, I used muscle testing to illustrate the power of positive words as opposed to the weakening force of negative words, and the value of good nutrition as opposed to poor nutrition. This was illustrated most dramatically while in the Olympic Village in Seoul, Korea in 1988, where I was a consultant.

While standing in line for food in the commissary, I noticed a tall, strong, vibrant looking man behind me. I asked him if he didn't mind me seeing how strong he was and to do a little experiment while waiting for food. He agreed.

He was a rower from the USA. I asked him to put his strong arm out, palm down to the side, horizontal to the floor. I placed the other hand at his thymus area of his chest. Taking three fingers of my left hand onto his right wrist, I said, "When I say 'stay strong,' resist my pressure." He was so strong that I could hang on his arm. (I weighed about 175 pounds at that time.) I picked up a packet of sugar, like some people put in coffee or tea, and asked him to hold it at his thymus and stay strong. I then pushed with my three fingers and his arm easily went down—as fast as his mouth! Taking the sugar from him, I gave him a packet of honey. I repeated the procedure, but this time he stayed strong because the honey is *natural* sugar and would assimilate into his body in a natural manner.

Continuing, I asked him to repeat to the person next to us, "I am weak," and to stay strong when I pushed. The result was he got weak! Switching the verbiage to "I am strong," he stayed strong. Then I did something that I'd never done before—I asked him to tell me his mother's name or to lie to me. I didn't know *his* name much less his mother's. He lied twice, getting weak, then stayed strong the third time, telling me the truth.

Years later, while presenting a Winning Ways workshop for the Cathedral High School soccer team in Los Angeles, a boy spontaneously blurted out a profanity. I had already demonstrated muscle testing, so I called him forward to see if profanity was really "bad" for you. He repeated a number of profanities as he tried to be strong yet he was weak. When I asked him to praise the students, he stayed strong! Yes, profanities are indeed "bad" words, and in more ways than one!

INTENSITY

Being intense in one workout doesn't bring intensity to every aspect of your big competition, but to be consistently intense in the moment of training is the one means of being intense throughout every competition and incomparable in the championships. This is true of studies for students, projects in business, and just about anything in life—simply apply intensity to whatever you do and want to improve. How can we be consistently intense in training? Let's look this over. **The quickest way to maximize your potential is to practice with the same intensity as you would participate in a championship.** Think of a time when you were intense for a complete workout. What did it feel like? What words would you use to describe the experience? Satisfaction? Inspired? Incomparable? Enthusiastic?

One of the major necessities for peak performance brought up at the Olympic training camps and clinics is quality training time. This has been expressed not only by the national coaches but by the college and professional coaches in every sport. Quality training time brings the habit of intensity to produce consistent quality performances. However, high school coaches noted that only few top natural athletes work hard each practice, and that some float along on natural talent. The elite coaches change this, requiring intensity at each practice, thus, bringing out the best in the best.

Stephan Curry, the great NBA basketball player, is often given as an example of a quality player who never just sat back on his great talents—he has performed superior-quality trainings, and therefore had great games. Stephan doesn't just take some shots in a lackadaisical fashion, he takes hundreds of shots from every conceivable situation and location on a basketball court. He practices shooting with someone in his face or even double-teamed. He practices intensely. He stays great through practicing what got him to be great—quality training time. Fanatics for quality training times include:

- Eric Heiden, who swept the speed-skating gold medals in the Olympics;

- Gale Sayers, the great Chicago Bears running back;

- Pete Rose, one of baseball's all-time greats;

- Haven Moses, Olympic and world record holder (400 meter hurdles);

- and many of the greats in all the sports.

How can you begin to intensify your quality training time? Isn't it difficult? If it were easy, everyone would be a pro or national champion. **The most successful in their sports make quality training time a *habit*.** And by your intensity in sports practices and trainings, you set a foundation which will carry over into your academic studies and vocation, enabling you to be all you can be. Attempt to give more than is expected and you will soon surprise yourself.

If you are not a competitor in sports, life is made out to be a big competition in America, *and* when you prepare for the little things, the big things are made easier and better! Whether it's an interview, a presentation, a sale, whatever, as *you* get better, your life is healthier, happier, and more connected with all.

USE THE FORCE

After a knee injury ended his own ultra marathon running in his 60s, Sri Chinmoy began lifting weights and within several years could shoulder-press more than 7,000 pounds on the special lifting apparatus (pictured below). He publicly lifted heavy objects including airplanes and pickup trucks to help increase awareness of the need for humanitarian aid. "His life was all about challenging yourself and being the best you can be," said Carl Lewis, the world and Olympic champion sprinter/long jumper, and a friend of Mr. Chinmoy's. "He told his disciples to go out and meet a challenge you don't think you can do, because you can do it with the heart."

Image: http://www.srichinmoy-reflections.com/sites/default/files/timeline/january/jan_30_87_7000lb_large.jpg

"Many of us remember the cold January New York evening, the structure was complete and Sri Chinmoy would not only have to raise the sixty-eight solid 100-pound plate weights, but also the supporting truss and bar, which themselves weighed an additional two hundred pounds. At 1:25 a.m., January 30, 1987, on his third attempt, Sri Chinmoy lifted 7,063¾ pounds. Of the five attempts (1:03 a.m., 1:13 a.m., 1:25 a.m., 1:37 a.m., and 1:50 a.m.), three were completely successful—a combined weight of over 10 *tons*, held aloft by one human arm and an unfathomable will. Jim Smith, from the British Amateur Weightlifters Association, who had been following Sri Chinmoy's progress since he began, put it simply: "Sri Chinmoy is causing us to throw all our current beliefs in physics out the window. Sri Chinmoy is wrecking what we've always regarded as normal laws. Sri Chinmoy is rewriting the physiology books all over again!"

—*Source: http://srichinmoy.wordpress.com*

BREAKING BARRIERS

My first experience of breaking an inch-thick, one-foot-square board was at the end of a weekend workshop by a prominent leader in personal development. He had us write on one side of the board face what was holding us back from success, and on the other side what it would be like to break that barrier. Most of us were successful that weekend.

One of my most fun and exciting moments using this "barrier breaker" was during an 8th grade combatives/self defense class. A young, short, skinny 13-year-old girl tried two days in a row to break the board, by hitting the *board* rather than hitting *beyond* the board. You could see and hear that it hurt her. On the third day, with similar instruction of hitting beyond the board, she easily split it, jumping into my arms, as the class cheered her success! Thank God that she persevered, following the dictum, "Persistence prevails when all else fails."

ENERGY FIELDS

I recall a lady named Betty Bethards, a dream analyst. She gave a public program with around 400 people in the early 1980s. In it, she exposed a way to enhance your energy field, to pump it up, if you will. It just took a simple wave of her magic wand. She would have been considered a witch in the old days, but modern science that can photograph people's energy fields, called Kirelian photography, now exists, which is a collection of photographic techniques used to capture the phenomenon of electrical coronal discharges. For ease of demonstration in these prehistoric-type times (the 1980s), she used dousing rods. As a person who supposedly saw people's electrical coronal discharges (auras) she pointed out a man across the large room. She said his aura was about three feet from him. Her rods directly pointed at him as she walked across the room. When she was three to four feet from the man, the rods parted without any movement of her hands.

Then as she turned to walk away, she casually raised her right hand up the center of the man's body from the waist to above his head. Few people noticed this. She went back across the room, looked the man over and said, "Your energy field just grew to about 10-15 feet away from me now." As she started walking back toward him the rods parted at the distance she mentioned! She had to explain to the audience how she raised the man's energy.

FIT AT BIRTH

"Precocious birthing" and "bio-engineering" are two items of current research which will enable performances that exceed the imagination. Fitness will soon begin at birth. The practice of *precocious birthing methods* will bring into the world more intuitive, intelligent, and physically evolved babies. Igor Charkovsky, the famous water birther, from Russia, allows children to be birthed underwater, then kept underwater while the umbilical cord is still throbbing, and stretches and contorts the child. Once the cord starts to reduce its throb, the child is raised to the surface, but is periodically bobbed underwater to stimulate the child's breathing. In our case, months prior to the birth of our first child, we were trained to cavort underwater together like dolphins. Periodically, we laid on nails, Mom from her hips to shoulders and I from ankles to shoulders. On the top of my torso were more nails with a cinder block. Further baby trainings followed after the birth with "tying Keith (our son) in knots, stretching its extremities in a yogic manner." The concept is that Igor moves the baby in precocious ways, which opens and develops the nerve/energy channels. He also had Keith (the baby) stay underwater for a period of time, sometimes bobbing him up and down, expanding his lung capacity to oxygenate the bodily system more than normal.

NOTE: Keith, without much training has been on two National Championship Club teams for the University of Colorado. I believe if he trained as hard as his dad, he could have been a regular Scholarship National Champion (not "just" Club). No parental bias here, of course!

The use of *bio-engineering* will soon create better muscle structures for optimum speed, strength, and endurance, for healing injuries rapidly, and much more. But BEWARE OF THIS! Acting like God is really chancy—just look what we've done with genetically modified organisms (GMOs) and what they have adversely created for the planet—*not good!* But studies and practices are now being applied in the Soviet Union and United States of America in these two fields. These will be described or applied for future investigations at another presentation on high technology and peak performance methods.

MIRACLES

A number of years ago I helped create a miracle! You can too! According to scripture, "If you had the faith of a mustard seed, you could move mountains." I tried it in South Africa while playing beach volleyball with the locals. A tall, talented man spiked the ball and came down wrong—you could hear a loud pop, indicating that he had badly torn his connective knee tissues. I dragged him off the court so that everyone else could play. I asked him if I could help and he gave permission.

I began using my skills as a teacher of practical sports psychology and my knowledge of anatomy, and I began guiding him through a detailed breathing, relaxation, and visualization process. It sounded a little like this: "Breathe in deeply and slowly through your nose. This brings the oxygen to the lower lobes of your lungs, where more of the air sacs are. The air sacs bring the oxygen to the blood. The brain is so smart that it sends more oxygen to the damaged area to heal it faster. Breathing out allows the damaged cells to be released."

At the same time, I gently placed my hands on his knee and periodically thanked God for having healed him. I had never done this kind of thing before, affirming that God cured the man, just like Jesus, the Master did. Within 45 minutes, *it worked!* He got up and walked away. I never even got his name. And this was not just a one-time event, either!

A number of years later, it happened again. A young man badly twisted and sprained his ankle while backpacking with a troop of Boy Scouts. He walked with a staff up to me. I did the same thing as I had done in South Africa, and it worked again! If I can do it, you can too. Just give it a go so that you can be a vehicle for someone's healing. It was a simple act of a little faith. Just attempting it, emulating the Master, except that He knew what the result was going to be, and I simply tried it, the "faith of a mustard seed" effect! From these experiences, I was inspired to take the scripture and use it and share it with others. How about you?

Acknowledgements

THIS BOOK COULD not have come about without the Spirit that animates life and has always prompted me to seek a higher, more sublime existence. Some people call it God, Allah, Krishna/Rama, Great Spirit, and some call it by other names, but by any name, the Spirit knows all, is in all and nothing, and is all-powerful. I am so grateful to feel it each day, to be guided by its promptings. Thank you. In saying this, I am also thanking you, the reader, because, as my greatest teacher, Muktananda Paramahansa said, *that Spirit dwells within you as you*. It has prompted you in some manner to choose this book and get what you choose from it.

Thanks to my parents, Chuck and Addie Krueger, elder sister, Karolynn and identical twin, Ken, who molded me into a young and questing man, affecting my life even today over 50 years since we lived together. I am most grateful to Muktananada, who was the initial inspiration for me working in the field of peak performance practices, and who instructed me to apply the teachings of Siddha Yoga and meditation to my daily life, and I have since 1975, when I began teaching meditation and yoga in schools and colleges. After my hijacking in 1977, I added teaching it as stress management for teachers and corporations, and finally evolving it into a program called Peak Performance Practices in 1981, teaching it with the Institute of Sports Psychology and Success Systems International.

My immediate family is the motivating factor in this mundane life. Thanks to Terez, my bride, wife, partner, lover, mother to our children, the perfect relationship for which I prayed. She created such an amazing home in which all is love and light, welcoming our great sons through her beautiful body and nurturing them into being all they can be as unique humans. As young caring adults, Keith and Narayan have their own paths to tread and may soon find their own callings and vocations.

There are so many compatriots throughout the years that have inspired me in integrating some of their wisdom and practices into my life. Among them, I wish to thank Dr. Gabriel Cousens, nutritionist/healer; Joseph Chilton Pearce, human developmentalist par excellence; Shakti Gawain, visualization maestro; Jim Clemmensen, compassionate educator/friend; Diane Tillman, author and practitioner of *Living Values: An Education Program* (LVEP); to the men on the various men's teams of the Division of Blood Soldiers, who prompted me to be the man I always wanted to be; and the world scriptures that inspire in provoking perfection, as in, "Be perfect as your Father in Heaven is perfect."

About The Author

A NATIVE OF LOS ANGELES, California, Kurt A. Krueger lives what he teaches and teaches what he lives. He set *three* school records while at Colorado University and coached the Water Polo Club that went undefeated in 1968. He has won 16 medals in four international Senior Olympic swim championships. Mr. Krueger has taught Peak Performance Practices (PPP) around the world for elite athletes and coaches, performing artists, business people, educators and students, and others since 1981. His goal is to have everyone physically and mentally fit throughout the 21st century. Mr. Krueger was an All-American swimmer and inducted into the Hall of Fame for water polo at Los Angeles Valley College. He also coached numerous world-record holders; was a member of Glendale College and California

State University Los Angeles faculties of psychology and/or physical education. He is an internationally published author, photographer, lecturer, and corporate consultant.

Mr. Krueger's interest in Winning Ways developed when he met Muktananda, a master of these sciences, in 1974. His integrative learning was tested three years later when he was a passenger on a Japan Airlines plane hijacked by the Japanese Red Army terrorists in Mumbai. Mr. Krueger used a super-concentration technique he'd been practicing and found his mind relaxed and focused at the height of the crisis, and was the first coach passenger to speak with hijackers and be released first!

Returning to America, Mr. Krueger taught social studies, history, anthropology, government, and economics at an inner-city ghetto school, Crenshaw High in Los Angeles. His mental control was again tested there when threatened by students carrying drawn knives and a gun. He peacefully settled the incident by verbally demanding the weapons. This clarity and ease in an intense situation amazed others as it did Mr. Krueger himself. Fellow teachers recognized his ability to cope with crisis situations and requested that he instruct them in stress management techniques. This ultimately led to a series of highly successful presentations in Southern California, culminating with a program at the United Nations in New York City and Oxford University's (UK) Medical School.

Mr. Krueger soon began training athletes for Peak Performance. It developed into a "systems" program to strengthen and tap a person's body, mind, and spirit. The use of these techniques has enabled him to win numerous medals in the international Senior Olympics. Some examples of high school student's improvements after less than three months' use of *Winning Ways* include:

- Greg Denby, a high jumper with a personal best of 6'6", leapt 7'1";

- Macarthur Osbourn went from a 2:01 880-yard runner to a 1:54;

- Anita Sood, Arjuna Award winner of India, set eight national swimming records, and

- Bejoy Jain, within 14 days of a workshop, set an Indian National Junior Record then swam the English Channel faster than any other Asian.

Mr. Krueger founded the Institute of Sports Psychology in 1982 in Bombay, which ultimately developed into an organization with four more offices in London, Melbourne, Tokyo, and Los Angeles. The following year he founded Success Systems International and developed programs and practices specifically for business and the performing and creative arts. Mr. Krueger has trained the Claremont Professional Football Club, Western Australia, which took second in the Grand Final that year (similar to America's Super Bowl). He has trained professionals and athletes of *six* different national teams. He has presented programs for the United States Military Academy, Young Presidents Organization, IBM, and other major corporations, as well as at major international conferences such as:

- A keynote speech, "Stress Management in Sports and Business," at the World Congress on Sports Psychology in Copenhagen;

- "Fitness for the 21st Century" at the Olympic Scientific Congress in Seoul;

- "Technology with a Heart" workshop at the International Conference on Technology and Education in Brussels;

- "Strengthening Character" at the American Alliance for Health, Physical Education Recreation and Dance Conference in San Diego.

He has been published nearly 50 times internationally in magazines and journals, and is a National Board Certified Teacher in secondary physical education, and is active with Boy Scouts of America. Mr. Krueger served on the Los Angeles Unified School District's Physical Education Advisory Board 2000-2014 and teaches Peak Performance Practices for the Academics and Sports professional development classes and workshops. He is currently involved in promoting Character Inclusion (www.linkedin.com/pulse/character-inclusion-kurt-krueger), and the World Fest (www.theworldfestorganization.org).

Mr. Krueger has done all of this with the singular purpose to create a more sustainable, peaceful, and prosperous world for all. Around the world, Mr. Krueger is recognized as a team builder, visionary, fitness futurist, sustainability stimulator, connector of complimentaries, and peace builder, and has achieved all of this while teaching full time for the

Los Angeles Unified School District in ghetto schools over a 47-year period. He retired—or "re-fired"—in June 2016.

Another Winning Way
Practice and Share!

DO YOU KNOW ANYONE who cannot improve? Yes, everyone is capable of so much more than they have imagined in their life. You now have a solid toolbox in which to dramatically advance in the quest to be all you can be while inspiring others to do the same, simply by your example!

1. Please, for your own benefit, practice a couple to a few of the Winning Ways right away. See the results for yourself, form a beneficial habit for your evolution, add more practices as you progress to evolve even faster. A key way to do this is through the Buddy System. Buddy Up! When you do receive rewards from your efforts in applying Winning Ways for Living in your life, Please email us your results. This always inspires others. You can also write a review on Amazon.

2. Sign up for our email updates that offer fresh videos and motivators to continue your quest for Winning Ways for Living. Doing this can add more happiness and healthy living every other month with simple inspirations and tools. We may also be offering a workshop in your state/country, which you could attend.

3. Many people learn through the visual along with the audible. To facilitate your evolution on your quest in life, I have set up a channel on YouTube: Peak Performance Prompters:

> https://www.youtube.com/playlist?list=PL-knXCX5m1O7puzZNOqaSxh7IfK6xv7Ga.

4. There is also an audile *Wining Ways for Living* coming out shortly for the visually impaired and an ebook available.

I wish you success in your quest.

—KURT KRUEGER, PHD – Play Happily Daily

www.successsystemsinternational.net

GET STARTED TODAY!

ABOUT THE INSTITUTE OF SPORTS PSYCHOLOGY

THE INSTITUTE OF Sports Psychology was founded in 1982 by fitness futurist, Kurt A. Krueger and the industrialist S. G. Somani. It was established on a holistic system to strengthen the body, mind, and spirit. The ISP is staffed by a group dedicated to enriching life by exposing us to our inherent potential. The institute's major goals are to:

- Research and present the most effective techniques and knowledge for reaching one's potential, and

- Educate elite athletes and coaches, professionals, performing artists, and people in business and industry through various programs and publications.

ABOUT SUCCESS SYSTEMS INTERNATIONAL

SUCCESS SYSTEMS INTERNATIONAL has been a leader in the holistic approach for creating amazing success throughout life since 1983. Sounds like too much glitz, but the proof continues in people's lives for those who follow the practices on five continents. We have worked with Fortune 500 companies from secretaries to their CEO's. It's also fun to work with schools at all levels in giving them concentration techniques and more for exposing students and teachers to their full potential.

Call or contact us if you want Peak Performance for all of your employees through:

- Team cohesion modalities,

- Fewer injuries and/or workman's compensation claims,

- Less illnesses through following nutritional and stress management practices,

- Fewer errors and accidents because of improved concentration on tasks and better managing of stress,

- Increased performance with creativity enhanced through happiness options and several mental and spiritual practices.

Government, business and industry, education, and NPO's all reap many benefits from our diverse programs.

Find out how we may custom tailor our life-transforming system for YOUR immediate success and long-term visions!

GET THE ULTIMATE IN ONE-ON-ONE AND GROUP IMPROVEMENT

Contact SSI today to find out about:

- Programs and presentations that cater to students, teachers, and other groups,

- Having Kurt speak at your next corporate or school event,

- Workshops,

- Retreats,

- The *Winning Ways Soundtrack* with special sounds/wavelengths for better concentration,

- International corporate consulting, and

- One-on-one coaching and mentoring,

Find out more and get involved at

SUCCESS SYSTEMS INTERNATIONAL

www.SuccessSystemsInternational.net

Or email: SuccessSystemsInternational@gmail.com

World Fest

www.theworldfestorganization.org

The annual WorldFest (WF) allows people of all walks of life to enjoy different music genres, diverse folk art, crafts, dance, performing arts of the world, and film.

Share the flavors of world cultures in food and drink. Hear inspirational visionary talks on peace and sustainability and the yearly theme for the WF. And experience the fun of co-operative games all the while bringing copious amounts of volunteers, money, and donations to quality charities each year.

Profits from the festival are used to expand WorldFest locations, with the majority of profits distributed to non-profits working for sustainable global solutions. Using the festival format, the WorldFest entertains and educates attendees to the possibilities of creating sustainable solutions to some of our mutual issues of survival—peace, justice, environment, and prosperity for all.

References

Primary Sources

Bell, K.F. *Championship Thinking*. Englewood Cliffs, NJ: Prentice-Hall, 1983.

Cratty, B.J. *Psychological Preparation and Athletic Excellence*. Ithica, NY: Movement Publications, 1984.

Diamond, H. & M. *Fit for Life*. New York: Warner Books, 1985.

Gallwey, W.T. *The Inner Game of Tennis*. New York: Random House, 1974.

Garfield,. C.A. *Peak Performance*. Los Angeles, CA: J.P. Tarcher, Inc., 1984.

Goleman, D. *The Varieties of Meditative Experience*. New York: Dutton, 1977.

Hass, R. *Eat to Win*. New York: Rawson Associates, 1983.

Herrigel, E. *Zen in the Art of Archery*. New York: Pantheon Books, 1953.

Josephson, N.F. "The Real Power Lunch," *American Health,* June 1985.

Kabat-Zenn, J.B. Bell, J. Rippe. *A Systematic Mental Training Program Based on Mindfulness Meditation to Optimize Performance in Collegiate and Olympic Rowers*. Paper presented at VI World Congress on Sport Psychology. Copenhagen, 1985.

Kagen, D. *"Mind Nutrients,"* OMNI *Magazine*, May, 1985.

Kauss, D.R. *Peak Performance*. Englewood Cliffs, NJ: Prentice-Hall, 1980.

Krueger, K.A. *"Meditation and the Ultimate Performance in Sports,"* *Sportsweek*, Bombay, September 5-11, 1984. Presented at the 1984 Olympic Scientific Congress, Eugene, Oregon.

-------. *"Meditation: A New Tool in the Sports Arena."* *Society of the National Institutes of Physical Education and Sports Journal*, Patiala, India: January, 1983.

Maclean P. "A Triune Concept of the Brain and Behavior," D. Campbell and T.J. Boag, eds. *The Clerence M. Hicks Memorial Lecture Series*. Toronto, Canada: University of Toronto Press, 1973.

Merrian, C. & G. *The Merrian-Webster Dictionary*. New York: Pocket Books, 1974.

Morehouse, L.E. *Maximum Performance*. New York: Simon and Schuster, 1977.

Muktananda, *Mukteshwari*. Bombay, India: Gurudev Siddha Peeth, 1972.

Murphy, M. and R. White. *The Psychic Side of Sports*. Reading, MA: Adison-Wesley, 1978.

Neideffer, R. *The Inner Athlete*. New York: Thomas Crowell Co., 1976.

Nityananda *"The Great Relationship."* *Siddha Path*. South Fallsburg, New York: 1985.

Pearce, J.C. *The Bond of Power*. New York: Dutton, 1981.

------- *Magical Child Matures*. New York: Dutton, 1985.

Pellitier, K. *Holistic Medicine*. New York: Dell Publishers, 1979.

------- *Mind as Healer; Mind as Slayer.* New York: Harper & Row, 1980.

Schollander, D. *Deep Water.* New York: Crown Publishers, 1971.

Shiarella, R. *Journey to Joy.* New York: Matrika Publications, Ltd., 1982.

Singh, J. *Sivasutras.* Delhi, India: Motilal Banarsidass, 1979.

Weindruch, R.H. *Federal Proceedings.* Vol. 38, page 418, Washington, D.C., 1979.

OTHER SOURCES

Garfield, Charles A. *Peak Performance.* Warner Books, 1984.

Harris & Harris. *Sports Psychology.* Leisure Press, 1984.

Hendricks and Carlson. *The Centered Athlete.* Englewood Cliffs: Prentice-Hall, 1982. A step-by-step guide for achieving balance and control of the body and mind.

Herrigal. *Zen in the Art of Archery.* New York: Pantheon Books, 1953. The life of a German student of a Japanese master of archery. A startling depiction for those interested in perfecting their actions.

Millman. *The Warrior Athlete.* Walpole: Stillpoint, 1979. Profiles the natural athlete within everyone, offering methods for accessing it.

Morehouse and Gross. *Maximum Performance.* Simon & Schuster, 1977.

Musashi. *The Book of Five Rings.* New York: Bantum, 1982.

Oh, Sadaharu. *A Zen Way of Baseball.* New York: Random House, 1984. A wonderful, if wordy autobiography of one of the most prolific home-run hitters in professional baseball.

Porter and Foster. *The Mental Athlete.* W.C. Brown Publishers, 1986

Schubert, Frank. *Psychology from Start to Finish.* Toronto, CA: Sport Books, 1986. Practical and psychologically oriented book for improving performance.

Shiarella, Robert. *Journey to Joy.* New York: Matrika, 1982. A clear and precise description of the inner journey, with methods for self-discovery.

RECOMMENDED READING
APPLIED KINESIOLOGY

Your Body Doesn't Lie by John Diamond

Behavioral Kinesiology by John Diamond

BREATHING

Body, Mind and Sport by Douillard

The Yoga of Breath: A Step-by-Step Guide to Pranayama by Richard Rosen

CONCENTRATION

The Inner Athlete by Robert Neideffer

Meditate by Muktananda

The Psychic Side of Sports by Michael Murphy

Inner Skiing by Thomas Gallwey

Sports Psychin by Thomas Tutko

The Bond of Power by Joseph Pearce

Pratyabhijnahridayam: The Secret of Self Recognition by Jaideva Singh

Play of Consciousness by Swami Muktananda

Powers of Mind by G.J.W. Goodman

In the Company of Siddha

Journey to Joy by Robert Shiarelle

Positive Addiction by William Glasser

MEDITATION

Siddha Meditation by Swami Muktananda

Wherever You Go, There You Are: Mindfulness Meditation in Everyday Life by Jon Kabat-Zinn

The Happiness Advantage and *Before Happiness* by Shawn Achor

Play of Consciousness by Baba Muktananda

Journey to Joy, Robert Shiarella, Matrika

Beyond the Relaxation Response by Herbert Benson

I Am That by Muktananda

The Inner Game of Tennis by W.T. Gallwey

NUTRITION

The New Laurel's Kitchen: A Handbook for Vegetarian Cookery and Nutrition by Laurel Robertson and Carol L. Flinders

Recipes for a Small Planet by Ellen Buchman Ewald

Your Body Doesn't Lie: Unlock the Power of Your Natural Energy! by John Diamond

Whole Life Nutrition Cookbook by Segersten and Malterre

Conscious Eating by Gabriel Cousens, M.D.

Staying Healthy with Nutrition, rev: The Complete Guide to Diet and Nutritional Medicine by Elson M. Haas and Buck Levin

The Virgin Diet by JJ Virgin

Physical Fitness

Runner's World Yoga Book by Couch

Hatha Yoga for Meditators by Dyananda

The Athlete's Guide to Yoga by Sage Rountree

The American Yoga Association's Yoga for Sports by Alice Christensen

Yoga Conditioning and Football by Coletto and Sloan

Positive Attitude

Maximum Sports Performance by J.F. Fixx

The Power of Positive Thinking by N.V. Peele

I Have Become Alive by Muktananda

Stress Management

Psychology from Start to Finish by Frank Schubert

Mind as Healer/Mind as Slayer by Kenneth Pellitier

Transform Stress Into Vitality by Chia Mantak

Superlearning by Sheila Ostrander and Lynn Schroeder

Journey to Joy by Robert Shiarella, Ph.D.

Muktananda: Selected Essays by Paul Zweig

Where are You Going? by Swami Muktananda

SWITCHING® HABITS

Books

Afformations, by Noah St. John

The Gentle Art of Blessing, by Pierre Pradervand

Nurturing with Love and Wisdom, Disciplining with Peace and Respect, by Diane Tillman

Practice of the Presence of God, by Brother Lawrence

Ties That Bind, by Dave Isay.

Websites

http://greatergood.berkeley.edu/article/item/stumbling_toward_gratitude/

http://www.gratefulness.org/books/

VISUALIZATION

Creative Visualization by Shakti Gawain

The Centered Athlete by Hendricks and Carlson

Sadaharu Oh: The Zen Way of Baseball by Oh and Falkner

Golf in the Kingdom by Michael Murphy

Beyond Jogging by Michael Spino

Zen in the Art of Archery by Herrigal

WARM-UPS AND COOL-DOWNS

Hatha Yoga for Meditators by Dyananda

Yoga for Beginners: The Daily Guide of Basic Yoga Poses and Exercises for Beginning Students by Michelle Nicole

SNIPES Journal at the National Institute of Sports, Patiala, India

YOGA

Beyond the Relaxation Response by Herbert Benson

Hatha Yoga for Meditators by Swami Dayananda

FINAL NOTE

Wisdom comes to you at a cost—not the cost of the book or this communication but the cost of *practice*.

Wisdom is worthless and you do not value wisdom and your life enough to apply what is optimum for you!

Implementing *Winning Ways for Living* is up to *you*, for *you*!

Foster Faith, Family, Freedom, and Friends!

How are you the Hope of Humanity?

How do blessings abound when You're around?

"Good is something you do,

not something you talk about.

Some medals are pinned to your soul,

not to your jacket."

—GINO BARTALI

WORLD WAR II ITALIAN CYCLING HERO

https://www.youtube.com/watch?v=U6vS1DuW5uM
(71 seconds)

Musical Ending

Life is like music, it's an art form

Some are composers

Some play music

Some dance to the music

Some like it and continue enjoying it

Some don't and either struggle with it or "drop out."

—Kurt Krueger, 11-7-16

Using the information and practices in *Winning Ways for Living* will enable you to be the composer of your life.

Using some of the information and practices will allow you to play more happily with the music.

If you didn't feel the information was provoking enough to take regular action for yourself, then you get to get the same old, same old.

The beauty of life is in its fullness!

Be the You that You want to be! God created you for a reason—find it and then give it away.

I will be donating a percentage of the profits from this book
to the Pachamama Alliance:

www.pachamama.org

Their vision is a world that works for everyone—an
environmentally sustainable, spiritually fulfilling, socially just
human presence on this planet—a New Dream for humanity.

47964960R10136

Made in the USA
San Bernardino, CA
12 April 2017